Ibn Sina's *Remarks and Admonitions:*
Physics and Metaphysics

Ibn Sina's *Remarks and Admonitions: Physics and Metaphysics*

AN ANALYSIS AND

ANNOTATED TRANSLATION

Shams Inati

Columbia University Press
New York

Columbia University Press
Publishers Since 1893
New York   Chichester, West Sussex
cup.columbia.edu
Copyright © 2014 Columbia University Press
All rights reserved

Library of Congress Cataloging-in-Publication Data

Avicenna, 980–1037.
[Isharat wa-al-tanbihat. Part 2–3. English]
Ibn Sina's Remarks and admonitions: physics and metaphysics: an analysis and annotated translation/
Shams C. Inati.
pages cm
Includes bibliographical references and index.
ISBN 978-0-231-16616-4 (cloth: alk. paper) —ISBN 978-0-231-53742-1 (e-book)
1. Islamic philosophy—Early works to 1800. 2. Philosophy, Medieval.
3. Physics—Early works to 1800. 4. Metaphysics—Early works to 1800.
I. Inati, Shams Constantine. II. Title.

B751.I62E5   2014
181'.5—dc23   2013041367

Columbia University Press books are printed on permanent and durable acid-free paper.

This book is printed on paper with recycled content.

Printed in the United States of America

References to Internet Web sites (URLs) were accurate at the time of writing. Neither the author nor Columbia University Press is responsible for URLs that may have expired or changed since the manuscript was prepared.

To my sister, Aminy Inati Audi, who has shared my passion for knowledge about the universe and the human place in it and who has supported my intellectual efforts and inspired me with her limitless determination, deep wisdom, and boundless love for all things.

Contents

Second Class: On the Directions and Their Primary and Secondary Bodies

Third Class: On the Terrestrial and Celestial Souls

Supplement to the [Third] Class:
On Expositing the Movements Produced by the Soul

PART THREE: METAPHYSICS

FOURTH CLASS: ON EXISTENCE AND ITS CAUSES

Fifth Class: Creation Ex Nihilo and Immediate Creation

Sixth Class: On Ends, on Their Principles, and on the Arrangement of Existence

SEVENTH CLASS: ON ABSTRACTION

Preface

Ibn Sina (Avicenna, A.D. 980–1037) is one of the most important medieval philosophers, and perhaps the most important philosopher in Islam. The wealth of philosophical and medical literature he left us includes books, essays, and poems concerned with the study of the cosmos with a special focus on nature, the human being, God, and their interrelationship.

Al-Ishārāt wal-Tanbīhāt (*Remarks and Admonitions*), which will hereafter be referred to as *al-Ishārāt*, is one of Ibn Sina's most mature and comprehensive philosophical works and one of the most important medieval philosophical texts. It is divided into four main parts: Logic, Physics, Metaphysics, and Sufism. I have already published an annotated translation and analysis of the first and last parts. Because the manuscript for the second and third parts was lost for several years, publication of these two parts was delayed.

In *al-Ishārāt*, as in his other writings such as *al-Shifā'* (*Healing*) and *Kitāb al-Najāt* (*The Book of Salvation*), the discussion covers a range of topics that primarily aim at understanding nature, the human being, and God. Building on logic, the gate to knowledge as Ibn Sina describes it, and preparing for reflections on happiness, the ultimate human goal, the *Physics* and *Metaphysics* seek to understand the natures of things, especially the human and the divine. These two parts explore, for example, the natures of bodies and souls, motion, change and

time, existence, creation, and knowledge. Of special importance is
the view Ibn Sina presents regarding God's knowledge of particulars,
a view that caused much discussion in medieval Islamic and Christian
philosophical and theological circles and provoked a strong rejection
by al-Ghazali. The last six chapters of the last class in the *Metaphysics*
are of great significance. They close with a discussion of providence,
good, and evil, a discussion Ibn Sina uses to introduce his theodicy.

The chapters in *al-Ishārāt* are short and usually titled either
Ishārāt or *Tanbīhāt*. Thus the title of the four parts, *al-Ishārāt wal-
Tanbīhāt*, is drawn from the titles of the majority of chapters. The
word *ishārāt* means, among other things, signs, remarks, indications,
allusions, symbolic expressions, and hints. Some of the meanings
of *tanbīhāt* are:warnings, admonitions, and cautionary advice. The
chapters entitled *Ishārāt* represent Ibn Sina's exposition of his own
views; those entitled *Tanbīhāt* represent his criticism of the views
of others and an attempt to alert the reader to the errors in these
views. Occasionally, the former are called "A Followup," "A Piece of
Advice," or "A Closing Comment and a Wish," and the latter "Delusion" or "Delusion and Admonition." The outcome is intended to
be a collection of concise yet complex hints at the truth clothed in
symbolic expressions plus constant brief reminders of where others
went wrong.

The aim of the present work is threefold: to analyze the *Physics*
and *Metaphysics* of *al-Ishārāt*; to provide an annotated English translation of it; and to amend the original Arabic text where necessary.
The book will, therefore, offer a detailed and thorough study of the
text, focusing on its central philosophical features, placing them in the
context of Ibn Sina's general philosophical thought, and determining
their source and place in the history of ideas. This preface is followed
by an analysis of the text, followed by the English translation of the
Arabic text.

The English translation is punctuated with emendations in [ ] where
the text is corrupt, missing information, or unclear, and with notes that
provide relevant and important references and further clarify difficult

points. Titles have also been added to all chapters to help the reader better understand the nature of the chapters and to allow me to make a meaningful table of contents. However, considering that all chapter titles following ":" are mine, and that this is pointed out here, no brackets have been added to chapter titles to avoid crowding the text with unnecessary marks. Page numbers of the Arabic text appear in ( ). The paragraphing and punctuation of the Arabic text have been changed to suit the English translation. Works cited in the notes without an author are by Ibn Sina. Arabic proper names of people and cities are transliterated without diacritical marks. All other Arabic words are transliterated following the system established by the American Library Association and the Library of Congress (ALA-LC Romanization Tables: Transliteration Schemes for Non-Roman Scripts). Finally, it should be noted that translations of passages from Ibn Sina's other works are also mine except where otherwise specified

It should be pointed out that the present work includes the first English translation and extensive analysis of the *Physics* and *Metaphysics* of *al-Ishārāt*. The translation is based on Sulayman Dunya's third edition of *al-Ishārāt, Part Two* (1992) and *Part Three* (1985). The Arabic text was compared at every step with Jack Forget's edition of *al-Ishārāt* (1893). In a few places, Forget's reading was adopted where it seemed more appropriate to Ibn Sina's thought than that of Dunya. M. Goichon's French translation of *al-Ishārāt* under the title *Livre des directives et remarques* was also thoroughly examined and was helpful in shedding light on certain difficulties of the Arabic text.

The technical terms are translated with deep sensitivity to their accurate meaning, which could not have been fully determined without also examining the text in light of Ibn Sina's other works and the commentaries on it, especially those of al-Tusi and al-Razi.

It is hoped that researchers, faculty, and students in philosophy, theology, religion, and intellectual history will find in this work a useful and necessary source for understanding Ibn Sina's philosophical thought and, more generally, medieval Islamic and Christian study of nature, the world beyond, psychology, God, and the concept of evil.

The preparation of this volume was made possible in part by a grant from the Translations Program of the National Endowment for the Humanities. Special appreciation is also due to the University of Pennsylvania and Villanova University for providing the facilities and library materials necessary for carrying out the project.

I am indebted to my sister, Professor Afifa Inati Haddad, for taking the time and energy to check thoroughly the necessary Arabic sources and to share with me her deep knowledge of the relevant aspects of the Arabic language. My sincere thanks must also go to Dr. Alison Anderson, Naziha Mustafa, Elie Saad, and Michael Fatigati for their assistance in research and patience in proofreading. Finally, I am grateful to the staff of Columbia University Press for the professionalism they brought to each stage of production.

Ibn Sina's *Remarks and Admonitions:*
Physics and Metaphysics

Analysis of the Text

As already mentioned in the preface, parts 2 and 3 of *al-Ishārāt* are respectively the *Physics* and the *Metaphysics*. The *Physics*, the study of nature (*al-Ṭabīʿiyyāt*), has three main sections, and the *Metaphysics*, theology or the study of that which is beyond nature (*al-Ilāhiyyāt*), has four. Each section is titled *Namaṭ* (Class), by which is meant a group of ideas.

It is worth noting that these titles are different from those of the main sections in the *Logic* of *al-Ishārāt*, which are called *Nahj* (Method). These two parts of *al-Ishārāt* also differ from the *Logic* in terms of continuity. While the *Physics* and *Metaphysics* seem to be intended as part of one work that includes *Physics*, *Metaphysics*, and *Mysticism* or *Sufism*, the *Logic* seems to be intended only as an introduction or instrument for the philosophical study that will follow and makes a sharp break with the three following parts: *Physics*, *Metaphysics*, and *Mysticism*. The continuity of the last three parts is evidenced by the fact that their sections are numbered consecutively as segments of the same series.

Thus the main sections of the *Physics* are the First, Second, and Third Classes; those in the *Metaphysics* are the Fourth, Fifth, Sixth, and Seventh Classes; and those in *Mysticism* are the Eighth, Ninth, and Tenth Classes. Also, like *Logic*, *Physics* opens with a prologue to indicate that it marks the beginning of a completely new study, but no prologue precedes *Metaphysics* or *Mysticism*.

PROLOGUE

After expressing reliance on God's guidance, Ibn Sina opens the work with a very short prologue, which includes an assertion and a request.

The assertion has a double purpose: to repeat an idea already presented in the prologue to the *Logic* and related to the nature of the work and to distinguish among people in terms of their intellectual abilities. As for the request, it specifies the manner in which the content of the work must be used.[1]

The assertion specifies that the remarks and admonitions of which the work consists are mere principles and generalities. People who are endowed with high intellectual sharpness are said to be able to understand and even detail them, as was made clear by the prologue to the *Logic*,[2] but those who are not so endowed will fail to understand even what is clearer than these are. Hence the request is made to protect these truths by keeping them hidden from those who cannot understand them. This request stems from Ibn Sina's concern that the work will be distorted and misused if it falls in the wrong hands. Therefore the request is to share the truths given in the work only with those capable of understanding them.

At the end of the prologue to the *Physics*, Ibn Sina states that the wish to protect these truths from those who cannot understand them is a repetition of a similar wish expressed "at the end of these remarks."[3] This statement may leave one puzzled as to which "similar wish" Ibn Sina is referring, since usually one repeats what has preceded, and the *Logic* preceding the *Physics* does not include such a wish, but only a distinction among people's intellectual abilities. However, I think the answer is clear and straightforward, because Ibn Sina specifies the place of the wish he is repeating, namely, the end of these remarks, that is, the end of the whole book. If this is the case, it must be that Ibn Sina went back and wrote the prologue to the *Physics*, or at least the last sentence of it, after completing the whole work. Here is the passage at the end of the work, which includes the wish to which Ibn Sina is referring:

> O brother! In these remarks, I have brought forth to you the cream of the truth and, bit by bit, I have fed you in sensitive words the best pieces of wisdom. Therefore, protect this truth

from the ignorant, the vulgar, those who are not endowed with sharpness of mind, with skill and experience, those who lend an ear to the crowds, and who have gone astray from philosophy and have fallen behind. Thus, if you find a person whose purity of heart and goodness of conduct you can trust, as well as his suspending judgment on that to which doubt hastens and his viewing the truth with the eye of satisfaction and honesty, then gradually, and in bits and pieces, give him the truth he requests, carefully observing what you get from what you have already given. Ask him to heed God and the inescapable faith, following your manner in what you give him and taking you as an example. If you divulge or lose this knowledge, God will be [the arbitrator] between you and me. God is sufficient as a trustee.[4]

Before discussing the *Physics* and *Metaphysics*, it is important to place these two branches of knowledge in the context of Ibn Sina's general philosophy. In *al-Shifāʾ, al-Manṭiq, al-Madkhal*, Ibn Sina divides philosophy (*falsafa*) into theoretical philosophy, which seeks knowledge of the truth for the purpose of perfecting the soul through the truth, and practical philosophy, which seeks knowledge of the good for the purpose of perfecting the soul through knowledge of what must be done as a guide for good action.[5] Theoretical philosophy is further divided into three branches: physics, which deals with things inasmuch as movement attaches to them in reality and in thought, such as humanity and horseness; pure mathematics, which deals with things inasmuch as movement attaches to them in reality but not in thought, such as squareness; and metaphysics, which deals with things inasmuch as movement attaches to them neither in reality nor in thought, regardless whether movement can attach to them, as in the case of unity and multiplicity, or cannot attach to them, as in the case of God and the intellect.[6] The subjects under practical philosophy are also in the main three: political science (city management), social science (family management), and ethics (individual management).[7]

In *al-Ashifāʾ* and *al-Najāt* the three branches of theoretical philosophy are addressed, but in *al-Ishārāt* only two of them, physics and metaphysics, are taken up. Pure mathematics is dropped out in *al-Ishārāt*, and mysticism, or what may be classified under ethics, is added instead. In other words, of the four parts of *al-Ishārāt*, the first (*Logic*) is not classified under any branch of philosophy (but perhaps only as a necessary instrument to philosophy or as the key to knowledge). The fourth (*Mysticism*) may be classified under practical philosophy. However, the second (*Physics*) and third (*Metaphysics*), which are the subject of the present volume, clearly fall under theoretical philosophy.

PHYSICS

Physics from the point of view of Ibn Sina is the study of certain principles and of things that attach to natural bodies. (The expression *natural bodies* in Ibn Sina's philosophy refers not only to bodies in our sublunary world but also bodies in the celestial sphere.) In the main, these principles are three: matter, form, and the agent intellect (the meaning of this last principle and the specific manner in which it is a physical principle will be determined later). Among the things that attach to natural bodies are motion and rest, time and place.

The First Class of the *Physics* is an inquiry into the substance or true reality of bodies and what attaches to it. This class includes thirty five chapters.

In the first five chapters earlier schools of atomism are discussed without mention of their names. Their concept of the uncuttable or indivisible part of which bodies are thought to be composed is denied. Ibn Sina believes that, though bodies are actually continuous, as confirmed by the external senses, they are potentially divisible, and their imaginative division, especially, is infinite. This conclusion is completed by the fourth chapter. Similarly, movement, which is the locomotive change of bodies, and time, which is the measurement of movement, are also said in the fifth chapter to be divisible to infinity.

Following that, evidence for the existence of matter is presented in chapters 6 to 9. It is argued that since bodies are actually continuous but potentially divisible, they must have the capacity for receiving division and continuity or disjunction and conjunction. This capacity belongs to something other than that which is continuous in itself by which is meant the corporeal form or the actually continuous by which is meant the body. The thing to which the capacity for receiving division and continuity belongs is said to be matter.

Chapter 10 asserts that quantity or corporeal form is joined to that in which it resides and of which it is a corporeal form. That thing is its matter, which in itself has no quantity, but is receptive of different quantities. Such a receptive thing is the first matter (al-hayulā al-ula). The intent in this chapter seems to be that since matter is capable of receiving different quantities, the largeness or smallness of the quantity of a thing is determined by how much quantity the matter of that thing receives rather than on anything else (be that internal such as void or external) such as an element adds to or subtracts from that thing.

Chapters 11 to 27 are devoted to a study of the relation of matter and form. The issue of whether or not the form may be free from matter is first discussed. Chapters 11 to 13 seek to provide evidence that the form cannot be free from matter—the reference here is to corporeal form. The argument may be summed up as follows:

No extension can be infinite. Therefore, corporeal extension is necessarily finite. Thus it is necessarily accompanied by shape in existence, though not in conception. Shape necessarily accompanies the extension either (1) owing to the extension itself and separate from matter; (2) owing to the impact of an external agent and separate from matter; or (3) owing to the subject or matter in which it resides. The first cannot be true; otherwise, "bodies become similar in the measures of extensions and in the dispositions of limits and shapes. Further, the supposed part of a certain measure would be necessarily accompanied by what necessarily accompanies the whole of that measure."[8] The second cannot be true either; otherwise, the corporeal measure becomes in itself subject to disjunction and conjunction and capable of reaction. But it has been proved that such disjunction, conjunction, and reactions are due to matter. It remains that the third is true; that is, the subject or matter is the reason for the necessary accompaniment of shape to corporeal extension.

In the following three chapters (14 to 16) Ibn Sina attempts to show that matter cannot be free from form as well. He asserts here that matter cannot have position; that is, it cannot be pointed to sensibly if it is abstract and that what gives it position is its linkage to the corporeal form.

Chapter 17 and 18 go further in attempting to provide evidence for the impossibility of matter being free from the specific form or from forms other than corporeal ones. Here Ibn Sina presents the following argument: "Matter may also not be free from other forms. How [could it be so free, when bodies] must be either: [1] with a form that necessitates the easy reception of disjunction, conjunction, and figuration; [2] with a form that necessitates this reception] with difficulty; or [3] with a form that necessitates the prevention of this reception. But none of this is required by corporeality."[9]

The argument seeks to demonstrate that the bodily receptivity for difference (whether with ease or with difficulty) or the receptivity for the lack of difference require something other than corporeal form and matter. This is because corporeal form is characterized by similarity, and so is matter. And whatever is characterized by similarity cannot be a cause for difference or the receptivity for that or the lack of it. In other words, since the receptivity for difference or for the lack of that in bodies cannot be explained by its being an effect of corporeal form or matter—because a cause characterized by similarity can only produce an effect characterized by the same—something other than corporeal form and matter must be responsible for the receptivity to difference in bodies. This is the specific form which is the form that provides receptivity for difference or the lack of it.

The factors determining the corporeal form are taken up briefly in chapter eighteen in what looks like a riddle. While pure matter is said to be a factor in such determination, it is also said not to be the only one. If it were the only factor, then "the already mentioned similitude [in quantity and shape] would be necessary. Rather, that whose states are different requires external determinants and states that work together in harmony to determine the required quantity and shape."[10] Ibn Sina does not specify here either the external determinants or the states intended. Instead, he goes on to say: "This is a secret that will help you understand other secrets."[11] Perhaps he desires to consider such determinants as a secret, because they include something from the world beyond. However, based on Ibn Sina's general philosophy, one may assume that "agent causes" refer to the celestial powers and "states" refer to prior forms that are individuated by matter, thus bringing multiplicity and differentiation to it and to the earthly conditions that prepare matter for the actual reception of the prior forms owing to the agency of the celestial powers.[12] Such conditions include natural transformations and forces.

The important issue of the relation between matter and form is further detailed by chapters 19 to 27. There it is asserted that the joining of form to matter is necessary for the actual subsistence or existence of matter. This means that if form separates from matter and is not replaced by another, matter becomes nonexistent. It also means that that which is responsible for the substitution of forms in matter is responsible for the existence of matter. Matter, on the other hand, is not necessary for the existence of form, but it is necessary for the existence of "things by which or with which the form exists."[13] The expression "things by which or with which the form exists" refers to shape and limit. Based on the assertion that matter is not necessary for the existence of form, Ibn Sina derives the conclusion that matter is not a cause prior in existence to form. He further argues that if matter were also necessary for the existence of form, when form is necessary for the existence of matter, then subsistence becomes circular, which is impossible.

The relation of body to surface, of surface to line, and of line to point, as well as the lack of the interpenetration of corporeal dimensions are then discussed in chapters 28 and 29, where it is said that the body, prior to its surface, and in existence not in conception, is necessarily accompanied by its surface inasmuch as it is accompanied by limit as a body. The surface is prior to the line and is limited by it if the body is in motion, but if the body is motionless, such as a sphere, its surface has no line. Similarly, the line is prior to the point and is limited by it if the body is in motion. But if the body is motionless, the line, such as the circumference of a circle, has no point.[14]

In chapters 30 and 31 Ibn Sina moves on to assert the impossibility of void, as did Aristotle before him. Contrary to a number of early Greek philosophers, such as Democritus, who believed the universe is made up of particles that swim in an empty space or void, Aristotle was of the opinion that no such space or void exists. Rather, the universe is a continuum filled with substance.[15] Ibn Sina's denial of void is based on the idea that disjoined bodies have distances between them. But regardless whether these distances are large or small, they remain estimable, and whatever is estimable is quantitative, and whatever is quantitative is not nothing. "Thus, if it were possible that such bodies have void among them and not bodies, then this void too will be an estimable distance. This void is not as some say 'a pure nothing,' even though it is not a body."[16] So if by void is meant pure nothing or nonexistence, then it is impossible to have void.

Finally, chapters 32 to 35 address the issue of directions in preparation for the discussion on directions in the Second Class. Direction is identified as a limit or extremity of extension toward which movement may be made. This means it has concrete existence and position. Because it has position, it is sensible and something toward which one may point.

The Second Class, which is on the directions and their primary and secondary bodies, has twenty-seven chapters.

By the primary bodies of directions is meant the bodies to which limit or extremity belongs. The secondary bodies of directions, on the other hand, are those whose existence with regard to direction is determined by the primary bodies.[17] If, for example, we say that John is to the left of Sarah, Sarah's body would be the primary body and John's the secondary one. However, if we say that Sarah is to the right of John, John's body would be the primary body and Sarah's the secondary one.

The first four chapters of the Second Class seek to prove that directions are determined only by an enveloping sphere, a single circular simple body that envelops all the bodies that have directions.[18]

To prove that there is a single spherical body that determines the directions, Ibn Sina first identifies six types of directions. Two of these, upward and downward, he considers unchangeable directions in nature. The other four types, which he describes as changeable by hypothesis, are relative in nature: front and back, left and right. This may be illustrated by the following example. If you are standing up in a natural position, above your head will always be upward and below your feet will always be downward. While you continue to stand in a natural position, what is in front and back of you and what is on your left and right may change if you turn around, while what is above you and below you remain the same despite your turning. Of course, you may stand on your head with your feet upward. But that would not be a natural position.

Ibn Sina then takes up the two unchangeable and fixed directions, leaving the other four aside owing to their relativity. He argues that the position of a direction must be determined either in a void or in a plenum. He asserts that it cannot be determined in a void, whether infinite or finite, because, in the first place, void does not exist, as shown in the First Class. It cannot be determined in an infinite plenum either, because the infinite has no limit, but a direction is a limit, as also stated in the First Class. Therefore the position of a direction lies outside void and an infinite plenum and can be determined only in a finite plenum. Ibn Sina then attempts to prove that this plenum is a single body. He argues that the delimitation of the two naturally distinct and opposing directions occurs either by, at least, two bodies or one body.

If the delimitation is by two bodies, either one of these bodies is inside the other or they are apart from each other. If the former, then the inside body is accidentally under the influence of the body that surrounds it. "This is because that which surrounds alone determines the two extremities of the dimension, by the proximity which is determined by what surrounds it and by the distance which is determined by its center"[19] Thus the body that is enclosed by another body does not determine the directions. Therefore the assumption that the determination of the two fixed directions occurs by two bodies, one of which is inside the other, is rejected.

If, on the other hand, the two bodies are apart, each body determines only the direction of "proximity" and not that of "distance." Thus the two opposing directions cannot be simultaneously determined by each body. "This is because distance from it must not be determined in a specific manner, unless [the body] is that which surrounds. Nor is the second [body] more fit than the first to be at a certain distance rather than at another possible distance, except due to [the interference of] an obstacle which necessarily helps in determining the direction, and which is corporeal. But the discourse involved in its supposition and consideration of its position is circular."[20] So the assumption of the two bodies apart from each other is rejected on the grounds of circularity as well.

If it is not possible that two bodies determine directions, then the remaining option is that determination of directions is accomplished by one body. However, this one body does that, not inasmuch as it is one (because, inasmuch as it is one, it can determine only one direction and not two distinct and opposing directions) or inasmuch as it "has just any sort of nature—but inasmuch as it is in a certain state that necessitates the determination of two opposite [limits]."[21] This required state is that it is enveloping, because if it is not enveloping it determines the proximate direction, but not that which is opposite this direction.

Ibn Sina asserts that the body that determines directions has position, but no linear motion or motion in place. If it were subject to linear motion, it would have to have direction. But that is impossible, because it envelops and determines all directions. Since this body

determines all directions of bodies, it must envelop all bodies Therefore it cannot have direction of its own; otherwise, it would have to
envelop itself.

This body is also said to be prior in existence to bodies that have
directions and are subject to linear motion. This priority is inasmuch
as this body is a cause for these bodies' directions and not inasmuch
as they are bodies.

Further, this body must be simple and without any parts in existence. This is because parts are prior in existence to the whole. But
it has been affirmed that the whole, that is, the enveloping body is
prior in existence to everything it envelops. Though this body cannot
have parts in existence, it can have them by hypothesis. Its supposed
parts must be uniform in relation to each other and to the center that
gives them position. If they are not so uniform, some parts become
closer to the center than some other parts. Therefore the positions
and directions of the different parts become different. This would
result in priority of direction to its determinant. This is impossible.[22]
Therefore the supposed parts of this body are uniform in position,
which means the body is circular. In other words, the single body that
determines the directions is not enveloping in just any manner, as, for
example, a rectangular body would envelop, but only in a spherical or
circular shape.[23]

Chapters 5 to 11 investigate some features of bodies and point out
first that a simple body is said not to require anything that is diversi-
fied, owing to its nature, which is undiversified in every way. The place
of simple and composite bodies is then taken up. It is asserted that a
body is to occupy one place only. (We have to assume that this is so
with the exception of the enveloping sphere, which, according to Ibn
Sina, has position but no place.) A simple body occupies one place in
accordance with the unity of its nature. A composite body occupies
one place in accordance with the requirement of the dominant part in
it. Returning to the simple body, Ibn Sina maintains that it must have a
circular shape "otherwise, its forms would be different in one matter,
[even though] they are the product of one force."[24]

It is added that a body has a propensity for motion, a propensity caused either by the nature of the body or by an outside factor. The natural propensity can operate fully only when the outside factor completely ceases. The stronger the natural propensity, the more resistant the body is to external or violent propensity. It is further asserted that the natural propensity seeks the object desired by the body's nature. This means that in actuality a body can have only one natural propensity that seeks an object; otherwise, a body might move in different directions at the same time in search of the desired object.

In the twelfth to seventeenth chapters Ibn Sina first asserts that the enveloping sphere or the body that determines directions has a circular motion on the grounds that it must have a propensity for circular motion. Such a propensity, he argues, must belong to the enveloping sphere, because, owing to their essential uniformity, the supposed parts of this body cannot occupy their positions due to their essence.[25] If so, they must occupy their positions by virtue of an external agent. Further, if they have an agent that moves them from one position to another, they must have a propensity for motion. For, as Ibn Sina argues, a body subject to violent motion necessarily requires a natural propensity of that body. Having established that this body has a propensity, he goes on to demonstrate that this propensity is for circular motion because no supposed part of it is more fit to be in a certain position than another.

He continues to say that, because its motion is circular, the object cannot undergo generation and corruption. This is because generation and corruption require a linear motion that moves the moving object from one place to another, not a circular motion. Generation is the appearance of a specific form in matter, while corruption is the disappearance of another specific form in it. In other words, the body susceptible to generation and corruption belongs to a certain species prior to corruption and to another species after generation. The enveloping sphere is never transformed from a specific species to another.

Following his consideration of the enveloping sphere, Ibn Sina now brings the discussion back to the terrestrial world. Chapters 18 to 20 take up a new issue related to this earth, namely, the number of primary bodily elements and the reason for their arrangement in their places.

The discussion boils down to the idea that while earthly bodies have many active and reactive qualities, there are only four primary qualities that necessarily accompany bodies. These are heat and cold, which belong to the genus of active qualities, that is, qualities that dispose their bodies to act on something else, and humidity and dryness, which belong to the genus of reactive qualities, that is, qualities that dispose their bodies to the action of other things. Thus terrestrial bodies act on each other and react to each other by virtue of the aforementioned qualities.

The bodies or elements that have the four primary qualities are four in number: fire, water, air, and earth. Fire is the body that has the highest degree of heat; water has the highest degree of cold; air has the highest degree of fluidity; and earth has the highest degree of solidity. These four bodies or elements have different forms; that is why none of them can be in the place of any of the others. In other words, these elements are arranged in places according to their forms.

Once the intermediacy of the elements in a mixture is reached, the mixture becomes ready to receive its specific form from the celestial sphere. It is said that the difference among the composites is caused by the difference in the quantity of the elements in the mixture of the composites. Such composites are asserted to be of three main types of beings: minerals, plants, and animals. The first type is without a soul. The second is with a soul responsible for nutrition, growth, and reproduction of the like, but without a sensitive part and without volition. And the third is also with a soul that has the aspects of the plant soul for nutrition, growth, and reproduction of the like plus a sensitive part and volition.

Generation and corruption in the terrestrial world are said in chapters 21 and 22 to be evidenced by the fact that the four elements have a common matter. The four elements are the fundamentals of generation and corruption owing to their common matter, which enables them to transform into each other. Thus the primary elements that cause generation and corruption are the principles of the completion of the things that have linear motion.[26] They are the fundamentals from which composites are made up and to which composites are reduced. Generation and corruption of the composites around us are further explored in chapter 23. They are viewed not as the replacement of the form by another, but as the replacement of the qualities or accidents that attach to it with other qualities or accidents.

Chapters 24 and 25 further elaborate the concept of change as involving substitution of accidents or internal qualities and responds to contrary views. Principles governing the nature and change of one of the four elements, fire, are taken as an example by chapter 26.

The last issue of the Second Class is covered by chapter 27 and deals with God's wisdom in creating the order of mixtures of the four elements and the impact of the degree of the temperament of the mixture on the degree of the perfection of the species. We are told that, because the mixture of the human species is closest to being balanced, the human soul is able to receive the rational soul, the soul closest to perfection. However, an unbalanced temperament of a mixture would lead to a deficient species. One cannot help recalling here Plato's theory of creation and how the Demiurge brought into existence different mixtures from which he created different species.[27] Here is how chapter 27 of the Second Class reads: "Reflect on the wisdom of the Maker. He began by creating principles from which He then created various mixtures. He prepared every mixture for a species, and He made the off balance of mixtures an off balance in the perfection of the species. He also made the mixture of a human being closest to the possible balance, so that the human rational soul could dwell in it."[28]

This also brings to mind al-Farabi's view in *Arā° Ahl al-Madīna al-Fāḍila*, where it is said: "Nonrational animals come into existence as a result of a more complex mixture than that of plants. Human beings alone come into existence as a result of the most complex mixture."[29]

By "the most complex mixture" al-Farabi means "the most complete mixture." This is the same as Ibn Sina's "most balanced mixture" and Plato's "purest mixture." All three expressions refer to the highest-ranking mixture reserved for human beings.

Contrary to the Aristotelian tradition, the *Physics* closes with a discussion primarily concerned with the soul. One may wonder why a discussion of the soul is included in *Physics*. It seems that the reason for this inclusion is that, according to Ibn Sina, the soul is intimately related to the body and plays a major role in the life of the body. After all, the soul is the source of motion in the body, the manager of the body, and two out of three parts of the human soul, as will soon be seen, belong to the body, in other words, to the realm of nature. Thus the last or Third Class of the *Physics* is devoted to a discussion of the soul and has thirty chapters.

The first five chapters attempt to show that the existence of the soul is grasped by intuition and that the soul is something other than corporeal.[30] It is said that, even in sleep or under the effect of drunkenness, the soul realizes that it exists, though this realization is not something that is constantly represented in memory. Here Ibn Sina introduces his famous "suspended person" argument (known also as the "flying or floating man argument") to prove that, independent of any sensory contact with the body, the soul enjoys self-awareness. "Further, if you imagine yourself at the beginning of its creation with a healthy intellect and a healthy disposition, and supposedly it is altogether in such a position and disposition as not to perceive its parts nor have its members in contact—but separate and suspended for a certain moment in free air—you find that it ignores everything except the assertion that it is."[31]

This soul, we are told, is not the temperament of the body, but the fundamental source of motion, apprehension, and retention of the temperament. It is the substance that manages the body and its temperament, as chapter 5 asserts. Chapter 6 takes up the important issue of the unity of the soul, the mutual effect of the soul and its powers or branches, which in turn affect their organs, in other words, affect the body.

The soul, which is asserted to be in reality the human being,[32] is said to be in itself one, though it branches out in the body's organs as faculties or powers. By means of these faculties the bodily organs and the soul affect each other. For example, one may become uncomfortable at hearing extremely loud noises, as one may shudder at thinking certain thoughts. Repetition of such effects may be the source of different levels of fixed habits that result in different levels of reactions. "These reactions and fixed habits may be stronger and they may be weaker. Were it not for such dispositions, the souls of some people would not have been, in accordance with habit, quicker than the souls of some others to become impudent and to flare up with anger."[33]

The notion of apprehension (idrāk) is introduced by chapter 7 and is defined as follows: Apprehension is having the reality of the apprehended object represented to the faculty with which one apprehends.[34]

In chapter 8 Ibn Sina discusses the various levels of apprehension on the scale of abstraction. It is said that a thing may be apprehended by the senses with no degree of abstraction when present to them. It may be apprehended by the imagination with some degree of abstraction where its form is represented internally when absent to the external senses. Or it may be apprehended by the intellect with the highest degree of abstraction, whereby its general concept, which is applicable to other members of its species, is apprehended. The difference between the sensible, the imagined, and the intelligible is pointed out, as well as how the last can be so either because it is pure in itself or because the intellect abstracts it.

Classification of the internal senses, the powers or faculties that apprehend internally, and their functions is covered by chapter 9. Contrary to Aristotle and some Muslim philosophers who consider the internal senses to be no more than three in number,[35] Ibn Sina considers them to be five. He first takes up the two internal senses that he classifies as most related to the external senses: the common sense (al-ḥiss al-mushtarak) and the representational power (al-muṣawwira).

The former is the power that corresponds to the external senses and apprehends the sensibles after they collect in it following their passage through the external senses. The latter is the power that stores the sensible images after their sensible objects disappear. While common sense and representational power distinguish the sensibles from each other, they also relate them to each other by judging, for example, that something like honey has such and such a texture, odor, and color. This they can do because the sensibles from the five external senses can be present to them at the same time as opposed to the way they are present to the external senses separately. "It is by virtue of these two powers that you can judge that this color is other than this taste and that that which has this color has this taste. That which judges these two matters needs to have the two things judged present to it together.[36]

Another internal power is estimation (al-wahm). It receives its objects, which are particular notions from external particular sensible objects. However, it receives them not through the external senses but through its own judgment or what one may consider instinct. Such notions are exemplified in the sheep's fear of the wolf. The objects of the estimative power are stored in a further power called memory (al-dhākira).

There remains one more internal power, which is given one of two names, depending on the role it plays. If it serves the intellect, it is called cognition (mufakkira). But if it serves the estimative power, it is called imagination (mutakhayyila; 382). It belongs to the imagination to divide and compose, separate and combine the objects of the representational power and those of memory (382). That is why its own objects are constructs of the sensible forms and the estimative notions. This means that, though the objects of the imagination are not exactly those of the representational power or those of memory, nevertheless they are like them in remaining particular and relating to the sensible or material world.

In addition to the plant and animal souls, the human soul also includes the rational soul, which is specifically human. This soul is a substance, which also has powers that are discussed in chapter 10. These powers are in the main two: the practical intellect (al-ʿaql al-ʿamalī) and the theoretical intellect (al-ʿaql al-naẓrī).

The function of the practical intellect is to manage the body. It does this by inferring "the necessary, particular human affairs that must be done in order to attain by this the chosen purposes from primary premises, well-spread premises, and experiential premises" (388). It is assisted by the theoretical intellect that provides it with universal opinions from which it derives particular ones (388).

The function of the theoretical intellect, on the other hand, is to perfect the substance of the rational soul as an actual intellect (al-ʿql bil-fiʿl; 388). It does that by employing the following powers or intellects which it possesses: (1) What may be referred to as the material intellect (al-ʿaql al-hayulānī), the power that prepares the rational soul for receiving the primary intelligibles. This is compared to primary matter in that it has no intelligibles, but has the capacity for receiving them. (2) The habitual intellect (al-ʿaql bil-malaka), which occurs to the soul following the occurrence of the primary intelligibles in it. This power prepares the soul for receiving the secondary intelligibles. It does this "either by thought which is the olive tree when it is weak, or by intuition which is also the oil when it is stronger than that" (390). In its highest degree the intuitive capacity is described as the "noble" and "saintly power," "whose oil almost lights up even without being touched by fire" (391). (3) The actual intellect (al-ʿaql bil-fiʿl). This is the power that acquires the intelligibles in actuality. (4) The acquired intellect (al-ʿaql al-mustafād). Though this is said to be a perfection, not a power as are the material, habitual, and actual intellects, nevertheless, it is also called an "intellect." This perfection provides the soul with the actual intelligibles whenever it desires to view them without any further effort.

It should be mentioned that the powers of the theoretical intellect do not fulfill their functions independently. Rather, they are aided by a fifth, nonhuman power, the agent intellect (al-ʿaql al-faʿʿāl). This lowest celestial intellect is said to transform the material intellect into the habitual one and the habitual one into the actual one (392). How it does this is not mentioned at this point.

Ibn Sina borrows Qur'anic terminology to describe the powers of the theoretical intellect,[37] perhaps to bestow an Islamic appearance on his view of the only human faculty capable of receiving knowledge of the truth. Thus, he calls the material intellect "the niche" and the habitual intellect "the glass." As seen previously, he also calls thought, as a means for acquiring the second intelligibles, "the olive tree" and intuition, as a means stronger than thought for doing the same thing, "the oil." "Lantern" refers to the actual intellect and "light upon light" to the acquired intellect. Finally, he retains the name "the fire" for the agent intellect.

Chapter 11 points out the difference between thought (al-fikra) and intuition (al-ḥds). However, since both thought and intuition belong to the habitual intellect, it would have been more appropriate to discuss them prior to or immediately after touching on the habitual intellect rather than in a subsequent chapter and after the treatment of the actual, acquired, and agent intellects. In any case, it seems that by "thought" Ibn Sina means the soul's movement from an unknown concept to a known one via a middle term. By "intuition," on the other hand, he means the soul's reaching of the same objective, that is, the known concept, but immediately and without a middle term. He confirms in chapter 12 that intuition occurs in degrees among people, ranging from the lowest or nonexistent to the highest or that which neighbors the surplus. "As you find the side of deficiency ending to the nonexistence of intuition, be certain that the side neighboring the surplus may end in most of its states to dispensing with learning and thought."[38] It is the state "neighboring the surplus" that Ibn Sina refers to as "the saintly power."[39]

The existence of the agent intellect and the conjunction of the human soul with it are discussed in chapters 13 and 14. Evidence for the existence of the agent intellect is said to consist in the fact that a thing in which intelligible forms are represented cannot be corporeal. (This is contrary to a thing in which sensible forms are represented in that it cannot but be corporeal.) Also, a thing in which intelligible forms are represented must be actual as the intelligible forms in it must be actual; otherwise, this thing cannot be a source and giver of them. Thus the source of intelligible forms must be a noncorporeal and an actual thing. Because this source cannot be potential to any degree, it cannot be a soul either. This is because a soul, inasmuch as it is a soul, cannot be in itself an actual but only a potential source of intelligible forms. Therefore the noncorporeal and actual source of intelligible forms must be external to us, since we are in part body and in part soul. This source is said to be the closest celestial intelligence to earth. It is the intelligence of the moon or what Ibn Sina refers to as the agent intellect or giver of forms (wāhib al-ṣuwar).[40]

Upon the conjunction between our rational souls and the agent intellect, intelligible forms in this intellect that suit the preparedness of our rational souls are then represented in our souls for the purpose of particular judgments. The conjunction is said to be caused by gradual preparedness for receiving the intelligible forms: first, by a potential power (the material intellect), which is a blank slate characterized by the general readiness for receiving the imprints of intelligible forms; second, by an acquisitive power (the habitual intellect), which acquires primary intelligibles that are principles for secondary ones; and third, by a power complete in preparedness for receiving the intelligibles in actuality (the actual intellect).

How the soul becomes prepared to receive the intelligible forms is addressed in chapter 15. There it is said that the soul acquires the preparation for this reception as a result of its "multiple managements of the sensible images and the intelligible archetypes that are in the representational power and in memory [respectively]."[41] So the soul's readiness to receive intelligible forms depends on its management of the sensible forms in two internal powers, the representational faculty and memory.

Chapters 16 to 18 maintain that the intelligible forms in themselves are indivisible and nonmaterial. That is why they cannot be represented in divisible and material things.

It is unavoidable that among the intelligibles there are indivisible concepts; otherwise, the intelligibles would be constructed only of principles that are actually infinite, even though it is unavoidable that in every multiplicity, be that finite or infinite, there is one in actuality. But if among the intelligibles, there is that which is one in actuality and which is intellected inasmuch as it is one, then it is intellected inasmuch as it is indivisible. Hence, [the intelligible] is not represented in that which is divisible in position. [However], every body and every power in a body is divisible.[42]

The conclusion to be drawn is that since all intelligibles are represented in the kind of place where any one intelligible is represented, and since, as shown above, one or more intelligibles can be represented in the human rational soul, it follows that all intelligibles can be represented in the human rational soul. This means that this soul and any other substance that intellects the intelligibles cannot be material and divisible, since what resides in it is nonmaterial and indivisible. The purpose of this argument is to show that the human rational soul is nonmaterial and indivisible. It should be made clear that by saying the intelligibles are indivisible Ibn Sina does not mean that they cannot be divided into universals, such as genus, species, and difference, but only that they cannot be divided into particular things in actuality. For example, while a genus such as animality can be divided into different species, for example, dogs, cats, and human beings, it cannot be divided into this dog, this cat, or this human being.

Chapters 19 to 21 advance the idea that every abstract thing is in itself a possible intellect (something that can acquire the intelligible forms) that, in addition to intellecting other things, intellects itself. This is because a thing that intellects something also intellects itself as intellecting that thing. Further, anything that intellects itself as intellecting anything also intellects itself.[43] That is, to be an abstract being is to be a possible knower, and to be such is to know and to be known or to be intelligible. It is worth pointing out that a thing that intellects is intelligible, but the contrary is not true. That is, not every intelligible is intellected, that is, if it is not independent of attachments.

Following a recapitulation in chapter 22 of what preceded regarding the intelligible forms, a short segment described as "Supplement to the [Third] Class" is presented under the title "On Expositing the Movements Produced by the Soul." This segment, which is intended to complete the Third Class, includes seven chapters.

Chapter 23 simply introduces the following chapters of the Third Class, which discuss the powers of the soul that produce the human actions and movements.

Chapter 24 is concerned with detailing the branches of the plant powers and their acts. These powers are said to be three: nutritive, growth, and reproductive. The plant movements or acts of nutrition, growth, and reproduction are involuntary and evidence the existence of these powers. The plant power on which the other two depend is the nutritive power whose life term is the longest of the three and continues to the end of the life of the individual. Contrary to that, the growth power terminates first among the three, followed by the reproductive power whose function is to preserve the species.

The animal powers with voluntary movements are the subject of chapter 25. The voluntary movements are said to have a decisive principle, which is acted upon by the imagination, the estimation, or the intellect. From this principle two powers proceed: the irascible and the desiderative. The former seeks harm, and the latter seeks what is necessary or beneficial for the individual. The demands of the former and the latter are met and obeyed by the muscular moving powers, whose function is to serve other powers.

Chapter 26 advances the idea that the propensity celestial bodies have for circular motion is evidence that this motion is animated and voluntary. In other words, this chapter is intended to demonstrate the existence of celestial souls.

Chapters 27 to 30 are devoted to the notion of volition. Chapter 27 differentiates between sensible and intellectual volitions and their objects. The object of the former volition is said to be a sensible notion, that is, predicable of one thing; while the object of the latter volition is said to be an intellectual notion, predicable of many things. In chapter 28 Ibn Sina asserts that the volition of the celestial souls, which are the source of the circular motion of the enveloping sphere, is intellectual, as is the volition of the human rational souls. In chapter 29, on the other hand, he investigates particular volition.

The Third Class closes with chapter 30, which argues that voluntary movement seeks what is best for the seeker either in actuality, in opinion, or in playful imagination

> for in that, there is a kind of concealed search for pleasure. The absentminded as well as the asleep act only when imagining a certain pleasure, a change in a certain weary state, or the removal of a certain illness. [While] the asleep imagines, his organs may also obey the movement resulting from his imagination—no doubt, in a state intermediate between sleep and wakefulness, or in a necessary thing, such as respiration, or in a thing that comes close to the necessary, as when one sees in sleep a very frightening or a very dear thing that may move one either to flee [from the former] or to seek [the latter].[44]

METAPHYSICS

In al-Ishārāt Ibn Sina does not specify what he means by "metaphysics," but in some of his other major works, such as al-Shifāʾ and al-Najāt, he does. In those works he says that metaphysics, which he also calls "first philosophy," "divine science," and "wisdom in an absolute sense,"[45] demonstrates the principles of theoretical philosophy through complete rational acquisition of these principles.[46] The subject of metaphysics is asserted to be the existent inasmuch as it exists or the general or absolute existent and the essential accidents, that is, the universals that necessarily attach to it without being part of its essence.

In other words, the subject of metaphysics is the existent, not inasmuch as it applies to some things and inasmuch as something particular attaches to it, as in physics and mathematics (such as quantity and quality, action and reaction, which attach to the objects of physics) but inasmuch as it applies to the principle of existence and inasmuch as something universal attaches to it (such as unity and multiplicity, potentiality and actuality, eternity and coming into being, cause and effect, universality and particularity, completeness and incompleteness, necessity and possibility).[47]

Metaphysics in *al-Ishārāt* begins with the Fourth Class, which is on existence and its causes and has twenty-nine chapters. The title of this class captures the spirit of its content and its major issues, existence and its causes. The objective here is primarily to distinguish between the causes of essence and those of existence and to prove there is an uncaused being that causes the existence of all other things. In other words, this class is concerned with the causes of existence, not those of essence. Once the existence of the uncaused being is demonstrated, its nature is then discussed in detail.

The first four chapters point out that existence in an absolute sense, the sense beyond the existence of this or that thing, is predicable of the caused and the uncaused existence, as well as the universals, quiddities, or primary realities of things that are intelligible and beyond the sensible. That is, they are beyond what is specified by states like quantity, quality, position, and place. Chapter 4 is characterized as a follow-up, because it reconfirms the idea that existence of a real being is due to the essential reality of that being and cannot be sensible. In other words, individual existents derive their existence from their essential or abstract realities. The First Principle, which gives things their essential realities that, in turn, give things their existence, must be an essential reality.

The fifth and sixth chapters distinguish between quiddities and existence and between their causes. Ibn Sina takes triangularity as an example of quiddities and considers its surface and lines as if they are its material cause (what makes a thing in potentiality) and formal cause (what makes a thing in actuality). In reality, the triangle has no material or formal cause, as these two causes belong to composite things, and the triangle is not such. That is why it is said "as if they are" and not "they are."[48] The existence of the triangle, on the other hand, is said to be caused by the efficient cause or agent (what makes a thing exist) and the final cause or end (what makes the efficient cause exist in terms of its efficiency to seek this end). In other words, a thing requires for its existence an efficient and a final cause, while for the realization of its essential reality it requires other causes, a material and a formal cause.

Chapters 7 and 8 elaborate the nature and function of the efficient and final causes, their relationship to other causes (whether or not embodying form and matter), and to each other. It is asserted that if there is a first cause it must be an efficient cause of everything else that exists.

Chapters 9 to 17 use the notions of the necessary in itself and the possible in itself to prove that there is a first cause that is uncaused. It is said that "every existent either has necessary existence in essence or has possible existence in essence."[49] The former exists independently of anything else, as its existence is due to itself. The latter depends for its existence on something else, as it has no existence in itself. Thus the existence of all possible things is from without.[50] However, the external causes of existence cannot go to infinity, because an infinite chain of possibles is possible and cannot become necessary except through another thing.[51] As this other thing causes the existence of the chain or totality of possibles, it also causes the existence of every possible in this chain or totality. Therefore, every chain or totality ends to a necessary in itself.

Though the existence of a thing is said to be an attribute of that thing,[52] it is different from that thing's other attributes. Other attributes are caused by that thing's quiddity, which is caused by existence or by other attributes of that thing. "However, it is not permissible that existence which is an attribute of a thing be verily caused by that thing's quiddity which is not existence, or by another attribute. This is because the cause is prior in existence, and nothing is prior in existence to existence."[53]

The nature of the uncaused being or the necessary in itself is portrayed in chapters 18 to 28. It is first said that this being is in essence one. Because of its unity, it cannot multiply in itself, but only in something receptive of multiplicity, that is, matter. However, in order for matter to multiply, it needs an agent that causes multiplicity in it. This is how the necessary in itself and matter differ in terms of the manner in which they multiply.

Because the necessary in itself is one in essence, it cannot be said of many. Hence it cannot be a species, as is "humanity" for human beings, or a genus, as is "animality" for animal individuals.

The fact that the necessary in itself is in essence one requires that its essence is also simple and indivisible. The argument for its simplicity and indivisibility goes like this: "If the essence of that whose existence is necessary is composed of two or more things that unite, it becomes necessary by them. One of these things or every one of them will be prior to it and a constituent of it.[54] Therefore, that whose existence is necessary is indivisible, whether in concept or in quantity."[55]

Additionally, the concept of the essence of the necessary in itself includes existence; otherwise, it would have to derive it from something else, since existence cannot be a concomitant of its essence either. But deriving it from something else is not possible for that which is the first and the uncaused cause.

The necessary in itself cannot be a body or dependent on a body either. To be a body is to divide into form and matter and to belong to a member of a species. But to be a body in either case is to be caused, which is contrary to being necessary in itself. Also, that which is necessary in itself cannot depend on a body, for to depend on a body is to be necessitated by that body and not by its own essence.

The necessary in itself cannot share in the quiddity of something(s) else. This is because the quiddities of things are possible in existence.

What about sharing in existence? To this question, Ibn Sina responds by saying that existence is neither a quiddity nor part of a quiddity, as it is never part of the concept of the quiddity, but simply something that occurs to a quiddity.[56] But that which is necessary in itself has no quiddity;[57] rather, it is pure existence. If so, that which is necessary in itself cannot share in existence. Because that which is necessary in itself has no quiddity and cannot share in the quiddity of anything else, it cannot have a genus. The reason is explicitly stated in al-Shifā', al-Ilāhiyyāt as follows: "This is because the First has no quiddity, and that which has no quiddity has no genus. The reason is that the genus is stated in the answer to 'What is it?' In a certain respect the genus is part of a thing, but it has been demonstrated that the First is not a composite."[58]

Since that which is necessary in itself has no quiddity, it cannot have any universal, which means it cannot have any species either.[59] If so, the distinction that is made among species or members of a genus by means of the difference is not needed in the case of that which is necessary in itself.[60] Though the necessary in itself is not distinguishable from and by other things, it is said to b distinguishable in and by its essence. Therefore, since the necessary in itself has no genus, no species, and no difference, it follows that it has no definition. This is because the definition consists of these three elements.[61]

The objector's expected question now is this: How about substance? Is it not a genus for that which is in itself, since substance is common to it and to other things? Ibn Sina points out here that substance is used in a different sense when applied to that which is necessary in itself than when applied to other things. In the former case it refers to actual existence as identical with the essence itself, not to an additional quiddity. In the latter case it refers to a quiddity additional to lower substances and in which such potential substances may share.[62]

Ibn Sina adds that the necessary in itself has no contrary whether in the sense used by the "multitude," as "an opposite equal force," or in the sense used by the "elite," as "that which shares in a subject consecutively and not simultaneously—if it is naturally at the extreme end."[63] The former sense is inapplicable to that which is necessary in itself, because it does not have an opposite equal force, since everything other than it is caused, while it is not. The latter sense is also inapplicable, because that which is necessary in itself does not share in anything or depend on anything.

It has been pointed out that that which is necessary in itself has no definition, because it lacks the ingredients necessary for a definition, that is, a genus, a species, and a difference. It has also been said that there is nothing similar to it, nor is there anything which is its contrary. The question remains then: How is it to be known? Ibn Sina states that, because it is indefinable, it can only be indicated through "pure intellectual knowledge."[64]

As he asserts in chapter 18 of the Third Class, Ibn Sina reiterates in chapter 28 of the Fourth Class that the First is an essence free from matter and any other extrinsic attachment additional to its essence. Because of that, it knows itself and is known by itself, since there is no impediment between it and itself. In other words, the First is a pure intelligence that mirrors itself and is mirrored by itself.

The Fourth Class closes with chapter 29, which concludes that evidence for the existence of the First, its unity, and its abstract nature is derived from reflection on nothing other than existence itself, as has been seen in the present class. Ibn Sina distinguishes here between two main types of proof for the existence of the First and uncaused cause: the proof derived from reflection on nothing other than existence in itself and the proof derived from the effects of that existence. The former is the nobler and more solid of the two, since its source is the First, the uncaused cause of all other things and the noblest being. This proof is advanced by "the truthful," by which Ibn Sina seems to mean "the philosophers." The latter proof, on the other hand, is less noble and less solid, since it begins with the effects of the First and uncaused cause. The reference here seems to be to the thing that is brought into existence from nonexistence by means of something else. This proof is advanced by a certain "group of people." These are the theologians and everybody else who seeks to demonstrate the First's existence from its creation.

The Fifth Class, which may be considered the core of the *Metaphysics* of *al-Ishārāt*, explores creation ex nihilo and immediate creation in twelve chapters.

In the first three chapters Ibn Sina refutes the view he attributes to the "commoners," by which he means the theologians, which asserts that once a thing comes into existence its need for the cause of its existence ceases. He says that they go as far as to claim that as the nonexistence of the builder does not affect the building he erected, the nonexistence of the Maker of the world would not harm the world's existence. He believes this view is due to the fact that those who adhere to it are of the opinion that an effect is used in one sense, namely, in the sense that a thing is brought into existence from nonexistence by means of another thing.

Ibn Sina analyzes the following expressions that represent concepts of acts: "fashions," "brings into existence," and "causes" into their simple elements in order to isolate a common ground among them."[65] He does this by stripping from them accidental elements, such as "through instrument" or "movement." The element that remains common between them is reduced to existence after nonexistence owing to another thing. So, apart from accidental elements, Ibn Sina finds that the concept of act as such includes existence after nonexistence. Therefore the concept of act includes existence, nonexistence, and existence as posterior to nonexistence.

The nonexistence cannot be "dependent on the agent of the existence of the effect," because nonexistence is nothing. Similarly, existence as posterior to nonexistence is not dependent on this agent either, because it is just a necessary attribute of this existence, as many attributes attach to possible things by necessity, owing to the essences of these things. It remains that the only thing that depends on the agent is existence and not existence in general. This is because the existence of that which is necessary in itself does not depend on an agent.[66]

The question Ibn Sina raises now is whether the existence that depends on the agent does so because it is possible in itself and necessary through another, or because it is posterior to nonexistence. He argues that that which is possible in itself and necessary through another is of two kinds: that which is not preceded by nonexistence—this is the necessary through another always—and that which is preceded by nonexistence—this is the necessary through another at a certain time. Therefore, that which is necessary through another is more general than that which is preceded by nonexistence. But if two concepts (one more general than the other) have a third concept in common, that third concept applies to the more general first and essentially to the more specific second by means of the former. This is because the third concept cannot apply to the latter except if it already applies to the former; while it can apply to the former without applying to the latter. From this it follows that dependence on the agent is for that which is necessary through another first and essentially and for that which is preceded by nonexistence second and by means of that which is necessary through another.[67]

The conclusion to be drawn is that since the world is necessary through another essentially, it is always dependent on its creator, and not only when it was generated.[68]

The fourth and fifth chapters are concerned with time, whose existence Ibn Sina asserts as evidenced by the priority and posteriority that belong to the existence of a thing. Such priority and posteriority are said to be due to time and are inconceivable apart from it.

The quiddity of time is described as nothing other than continuity of passage and renewal, a kind of continuity that is not divisible except mentally. Therefore it has no actual parts and has no priority and posteriority before division. In chapter 5 Ibn Sina defines time as a quantity that measures change, that is, motion, not in terms of distance but in terms of priority and posteriority, which do not meet.[69] (Priority and posteriority do meet in terms of distance, but not in terms of time.)

Chapters 6 to 8 take up the topic of possible things and assert that whatever begins to exist is possible in existence before existing and cannot but be in a subject or matter. If it were not possible before existing, it would have to be impossible. But if it were impossible, it could not come into existence. Its possibility is in itself conceptual or intelligible and in relation to the existence of a thing. Possibility, therefore, is a relative thing. Because relative things are accidents, and accidents cannot but be in a subject, possibility cannot but be in a subject.

The existence of a thing that is preceded by possibility is posterior to the possibility essentially and not in time. That which is possible in itself and necessary through another becomes nonexistent concretely if it separates from that other (but remains indifferent to existence mentally). This is because a thing exists concretely inasmuch as its cause or that other exists and is in the state of causation of existence,

> such as the state of nature, volition, or some further thing that must be one of the external things that take part in the completion of the cause as an actual cause. Such things are exemplified by [1] the instrument, [as in] the carpenter's need for the hammer; [2] the matter, [as in] the carpenter's need for wood; [3] the assistant, [as in] the sawyer's need for another sawyer; [4] the time, [as in] a human being's need for the summer; or [6] the removal of an obstacle, [as in] the washer's need for the removal of heavy rain.[70]

However, if the cause of that other does not exist or is not in the state of causation of existence, then its effect does not exist concretely.

The concept of immediate creation (al-ibdāʿ) is defined in chapter 9 as giving existence to another thing "without the mediation of matter, instrument, or time."[71] In contrast, temporal creation, for example, requires the mediation of an instrument to bring a thing from temporal nonexistence to temporal existence. Any production preceded by time and matter is preceded by nonexistence. Ibn Sina wishes to demonstrate the contrary of this: "Whatever is not preceded by matter and time is not preceded by nonexistence."[72] The latter is immediate creation, which is said to be nobler than temporal and material creation. No reason for that is given, but this seems to be a conclusion of the above, namely, that immediate creation does not require an instrument, is not preceded by nonexistence, and belongs to the First. On the other hand, temporal and material creation requires an instrument, is preceded by nonexistence, and belongs to what is distant from the First.

In chapter 10 Ibn Sina returns to the investigation of the existence of whatever is possible in itself. Such a thing, he asserts, becomes necessary only through its cause. In order for the possible to exist, it needs a cause whose necessary causation tips the existence of that possible over its nonexistence.

In chapters 11 and 12 Ibn Sina moves on to demonstrate that the truly one, inasmuch as it is one, cannot necessitate except the existence of one thing. This is because if the One were to produce two things it would include a duality of causation or aspects. But that is impossible for that which is truly one.

Chapter 12 also discusses various views regarding the issues of necessity and possibility, as well as eternity and generation, presenting, at the same time, Ibn Sina's response to these views.

The Sixth Class is on ends, their principles, and the arrangement of existence and consists of forty-two chapters. As the title of this class indicates, the objective here is exploration of three major issues: ends (objects chosen over other things for being considered by the choice maker better and more needed than those things),[73] their principles (intellects), and the order of existence.

Having felt that he had already demonstrated in the Fourth Class the existence of a first principle and the manner of creation in the Fifth Class, Ibn Sina now turns his attention to the nature of this principle. In the first eight chapters he investigates whether it is possible for the First and other exalted beings to seek something in things lower than they are. To begin with, he denies the First this possibility on the ground that it is fully rich or completely independent in essence and disposition. He defines the rich as that which is independent of other things in three ways: "in its essence, in dispositions that take hold of its essence and in perfective dispositions in relation to its essence."[74]

This definition is introduced to show that the First Principle is rich in every way and in an absolute sense, as it is independent of everything. Since a thing seeks another out of lack or poverty of something better in essence or in some kind of disposition, and since the First is not lacking or "poor" in any way, for it is absolutely rich, it cannot seek anything. In other words, the First does not perform any act for the purpose of fulfilling itself, because it is already rich and does not need anything or for the purpose of other things, because, in the first place, it cannot seek to do anything for the purpose of anything else. Al-Najāt explains the reason as follows: "Every intention is for the sake of the intended and is less in existence than the intended. This is because whatever is an end for something else is more complete in existence than that other. . . . It is not permissible that the more complete existence be derived from that which is baser."[75]

Other exalted things are also said not to do anything for the sake of lower things: "How abominable it is to say then that exalted things try to do something for what is below them since that is better for them, and in order to be agents of good deeds since that is among what is good and appropriate for noble things."[76]

In short, the idea is that a thing seeks what it considers better for it in some way. Exalted things, including the First, have nothing to seek in things lower than they are, as the lower things have nothing better than what the exalted things possess.

Ibn Sina is aware that the following question will immediately come to the mind of the opponent: if that is the case, then why do exalted beings, including the First, do things that are good for lower beings? Ibn Sina's response is that they do so only out of generosity. By "generosity," he means doing something that must be (yanbaghî),[77] but without compensation of any sort: "Therefore, perhaps one who gives the knife to him who must not have it is not generous. Also, one who gives in order to obtain a compensation from him with whom one is dealing is not generous."[78]

Because of its absolute richness and full independence, the First is crowned as the "real king" that does not depend on anything, but on which everything else depends: "The real king is the absolutely real rich and the one with which nothing can dispense in any matter, and the one to which the essence of everything belongs. This is because everything is from it or is among those things whose essence is from it."[79]

In chapter 9, Ibn Sina prepares the way for the discussion of the universal order of existence and providence that will follow. He briefly points out that this order with its necessary time is represented in divine knowledge from which it flows in detail. He calls the flow of divine knowledge into the universe "providence,"[80] as did Plotinus before him.[81]

It is worth noting here that, to Ibn Sina, following the First in existence, the hierarchy of existence and perfection of being consists of the celestial and then the terrestrial spheres. In the former the intellects come first, then the souls, and then the bodies. The following five chapters, 10 to 14, are focused on the existence of and relation among the celestial intellects, souls, and bodies, the celestial motion, and the human ability to grasp all of that.

As pointed out in the Third Class, the celestial motions are said to be dependent on a universal volition and a particular one.[82] The particular volition, we are told, is determined "by a particular thing that brings it into being. The universal volition corresponds to a universal sought object for which it is not necessary to have specification or particularization."[83] It is further added that "the principle of the universal and absolute first volition must be a separate intellectual essence. If this volition perfects [its] substance by its own virtue, it will not be accompanied by insufficiency. Thus it will be a volition resembling the already mentioned providence"[84] In other words, the principle of a universal volition must be a separate intellect, because universality cannot be grasped by material things. Being free from materiality, such an intellect is pure and compared to the divine providence.

Further, all universal or nonmaterial things are permanent, and all perfections of permanent things, including separate intellects, are continuous and real. The opposite of these qualities belong to material things, including the intellects.

The volition of the celestial souls, on the other hand, is either particular or universal. It is by virtue of the latter that these souls seek to perfect themselves. Ibn Sina classifies as "a mystery" the celestial souls' possession of universal volition.[85] He does not give a reason, but perhaps this classification is because, to him, a thing usually has one type of volition, not two as do the celestial souls.

Based on what has preceded, the celestial intellects, being the purest, most complete, and highest among celestial things, must not be able to desire or seek the celestial souls and bodies that are less pure, less complete, and lower than they are. The celestial souls, on the other hand, can and do desire and seek the celestial intellects and move to imitate them in essence or in some state through moving the celestial bodies. Thus, the celestial intellects are the principles of celestial motion, not in that they directly move the heavens or are its efficient causes, but in that they are its indirect movers and final causes by being the objects the celestial souls desire and that cause the celestial motions to fulfill their own desires for perfection. Therefore the celestial intellects are the primary, remote, or indirect movers of the heavens, while the celestial souls are its secondary, proximate, and direct movers.

Chapters 12 and 13 assert that the resembled objects of the celestial bodies are things different in number. But, because the first resembled object is one,[86] the movements of the celestial bodies must be circular. If simple bodies are left to "their natures and their natural shapes, they would be circular. This is because the natural shape of simple bodies is circular."[87] Also, movable simple bodies that are left to their natures "must necessarily have principles for certain circular movements."[88] The first resembled object that moves the celestial bodies is a final but not an efficient cause of the celestial movements.

The resemblance of the celestial moved objects to their movers is something that, Ibn Sina says, may be known by the human mind only in general. The reason is that human mental capacity is incapable of grasping what is even closer to it than what belongs to the celestial realm. However, if a human being makes an effort at reflection on the human soul, a secret may be revealed regarding the immateriality of the celestial souls. With this we come to the end of the discussion of ends and their principles.

Chapters 14 to 23 lead to the conclusion expressed in chapter 24 and further defended in chapters 25 to 28, namely, that the force moving the celestial sphere is noncorporeal, infinite, separate, and intellectual. The idea is that celestial movers move their celestial bodies in an infinite way, and that infinite movement cannot be by means of a corporeal power. This is why celestial movers are noncorporeal, infinite, and separate substances. In support of his argument that the celestial movers are noncorporeal, Ibn Sina cites Aristotle's view: "The father of Peripatetics had attested that the mover of every sphere emits [to that sphere] an infinite movement and that its force is infinite; [therefore] it is not in a corporeal force."[89]

Chapters 29 to 36 focus primarily on causation of celestial principles and bodies. The first of the movers is asserted to be the First Principle, the noncaused being, which is one and free from aspects. This means that it can be a principle for a simple thing only and cannot be a principle for nonsimple things except by mediation. The principle produced by the First, however, can have a duality of aspects. This first-caused principle is what Plotinus calls *nous* and also attributes to it multiplicity. Plotinus gives two reasons as to the source of multiplicity in this principle: (1) because there are to it at least two aspects—its reflection upon its source and its reflection upon itself; and (2) because it includes all the ideas or forms, not only those admitted by Plato but others as well.[90]

Because a body is made up of matter and form, it cannot be produced by the First directly, but only through the mediation of something that has a duality of aspects. Ibn Sina seeks to prove here that the

First Cause cannot be a body; rather, it is a separate intellect. Further, the first-caused principle or the direct effect of the First Principle is also a noncorporeal and separate intellect, which is the first in the series of celestial intellects.

Owing to their dual natures, celestial bodies cannot be caused by the First Principle directly. Nor can they be caused by each other or by their corporeal forms or souls, as chapter 36 concludes.

> Bodies act only by their forms, and the forms that subsist in the bodies, and which are the perfections of those bodies, produce their actions only by the mediation of that by virtue of which they subsist. The body does not mediate between a [complete] thing and that which is not a body—be that matter or form—such that it makes both of them exist first, and then from both of them, it makes the body exist. Therefore, corporeal forms are not causes either of the matters or of the forms of bodies.[91]

Therefore, celestial bodies are caused neither by bodies nor by corporeal forms or souls, nor, of course, by the First Principle. It remains that they must be caused by separate principles other than the First. Such principles are the separate celestial intellects, as chapter 37 shows.

Building, in part, on what has been advanced, the discussion in chapters 37 to 42 focuses on the arrangement of existents and concludes the following:

(1) The First Intellectual Principle or the necessary in itself is one and is not predicable of any genus or species.
(2) Because the First Principle is one and free from all aspects, it cannot produce directly or immediately except something that is also one.
(3) The only thing the First Principle causes directly or immediately is by virtue of reflecting on itself.

(4) The first caused principle is like its cause, intellectual, separate, and one, because its cause is void of a multiplicity of aspects. But it is different from its cause in that it is characterized by a number of aspects of reflection.

(5) The aspects of the first caused principle are reflection on its cause as necessary in itself; reflection on itself as necessary through another, that is, as a necessary effect of the First Principle; and reflection on itself as possible in itself.

(6) By virtue of reflection on its cause, the first caused principle produces another intellectual principle. By virtue of reflection on its being a necessary effect of its cause, it produces the first celestial soul. And by virtue of reflection on its being possible in itself, it produces the first celestial body.

(7) The second celestial intellectual principle also produces three things: an intellectual principle as it reflects on its cause, a celestial soul as it reflects on itself as necessary through its cause, and a celestial body as it reflects on its being possible in itself.

(8) The process of celestial production continues until it ends with the last celestial intellectual principle or what is called the agent intellect. This intellect does not produce any celestial soul or body, owing to its high level of intellectual dimness, considering its long distance from the original source of intellectual being. Rather, this intellect produces our terrestrial world of elements and the human rational soul.

In other words, owing to its multiple nature, the first caused principle is responsible for the multiplicity of the remaining celestial intellectual principles, souls, and bodies, as well as the terrestrial intellectual principles, souls, and bodies. In this it mediates between the First principle and the rest of existence. Ibn Sina sums up the immediate creation of the first caused intellect and the mediated creation of the other celestial intellects and bodies as follows: "Thus, the First creates an intellectual substance which is in truth created, and by the mediation of this substance, creates another substance and a celestial body. The same is created from the [latter] intellectual substance. [This goes on] until the celestial bodies are completed. This leads to an intellectual substance from which no celestial body necessarily follows."[92]

With the last chapter in the story of creation, Ibn Sina closes the Sixth Class. There it is asserted that the formation of our world is a necessary result of the last celestial intellectual substance or the agent intellect aided by the celestial bodies.

We are told that the agent intellect assisted by celestial bodies necessarily emanates into the matter of the world of generation and corruption. To give stability to this necessary emanation of matter, the agent intellect also bestows forms on the different matters, according to the difference in preparation for form reception of these matters.

This difference in preparation is attributed to "the celestial bodies by virtue of separating what surrounds the central region from what surrounds the enveloping region, and of dispositions whose details are much too sensitive to be grasped by [human] minds, even though such minds discern their generalities."[93]

Among the forms that emanate from the agent intellect are the plant souls, the animal souls, and the human rational souls—the last being the final existents in the hierarchy of intellectual substances. If the human rational souls are to perfect themselves, they need to employ bodily instruments, such as the senses, and to receive the assistance of the agent intellect in bestowing its forms on them. It should be noted here that, according to Ibn Sina's general philosophy, perfecting the human rational souls requires the use of bodily instruments only in the case of philosophers. In the case of prophets, only the agent intellect is needed to illuminate these souls with its forms.

The Seventh Class, which is on abstraction (purity from matter and potentiality) and which includes twenty-seven chapters, picks up where the Sixth Class left off.

After describing the descent of existence from the First Principle or total simplicity and unity to matter, or the ultimate source of multiplicity as the descent from the noblest to the basest, Ibn Sina describes the way back as the ascent from the basest to the noblest. He gives special attention to an essential point on the way of return, namely, the last and highest entity that comes into existence, the human rational soul and its highest rank, the acquired intellect, which includes the forms of all existing things.

The first six chapters discuss the independence of the rational soul from the body. This soul, Ibn Sina asserts, is independent from the body in existence and dependent only on its causes, the eternal substances. Though it uses the body as its instrument, it is not part of the body, but simply subsists in it. As such, the death of the body does not affect its existence.[94]

Not only is the rational soul's existence asserted to be unaffected by the death of its body, its intellection is also said to be independent of the body and unharmed by this loss, if the rational soul had already acquired the habit of conjunction with the agent intellect. The reason is that once the rational soul reaches the acquired intellect, it knows by itself and without any reference to the body.[95]

Ibn Sina points out that if the rational soul intellects by means of its bodily instruments, it becomes fatigued whenever the bodily instruments it uses are fatigued. But this is not the case. He adds that, contrary to bodily faculties, such as the sensitive and locomotive powers, that are fatigued by bodily fatigue, the rational soul is unaffected by bodily fatigue. This, he asserts, proves that the rational soul is independent of the body.

He further observes that it often happens that while some bodily powers, such as the sensitive and locomotive powers, weaken and even disintegrate, the powers of the rational soul remain of the same strength or even develop further.[96]

Additionally, he argues that even if the rational soul experiences fatigue at the same time the body is undergoing the same experience, it does not follow that the soul does not act independently. He clarifies this point by saying, "something from without may occur to a thing and distract it from its acts by itself. But this does not show that the latter thing has no acts by itself. However, if this thing exists, [if] it is not distracted by something else, and [if] it has no need for something else, then this shows that it has acts by itself."[97]

In support of his view that the rational soul is independent of the body, Ibn Sina also offers the following arguments:

While bodily powers are fatigued by the repetition of acts, especially if they are strong acts, this is not the case with regard to the acts of the rational soul. In the case of the repetition of bodily acts, the weak act is almost "unnoticed" after a repeated act, especially if this act is strong. This is exemplified in looking at a dim light after repeatedly looking at a strong one. "The acts of the rational power may often be the opposite of what has been described [previously]."[98]

Moreover, Ibn Sina holds that whatever apprehends by means of a bodily instrument, as do the sensitive powers, cannot apprehend itself, its apprehensions, or its instrument. This is because it cannot have an instrument between itself and these things. But, without an instrument, it cannot apprehend anything. Since the rational soul can apprehend itself, its apprehension, and its instrument, its apprehension cannot be by means of a bodily instrument.

Finally, Ibn Sina argues that if the rational soul were imprinted in a body it would either have permanent knowledge of that body or no knowledge of it. His reasoning is this. For the soul to know is for it to grasp the form of the known object. This is to say, if the soul is to know its body, it has to grasp the form of that body. But if it is imprinted in the body, it is material and already has a form. Therefore, if the rational soul comes to know the body, it will have two forms, which Ibn Sina argues is impossible.

Because this power is material, it is necessary that what it acquires, such as the form of the known object that comes from the matter of this object, also exist in its matter. Because the acquisition [of the form] of the known object is renewed, it is other than the form which has not ceased numerically to be for it in its matter and for its matter. Thus, two forms for one thing would be acquired simultaneously in one matter which is enveloped by the accidents of its individuals. But the falsehood of this has already been demonstrated. Hence, the form by virtue of which the rational power becomes intellective of its instruments is the form of the thing in which the rational power is found and [by virtue of which] this power is always joined to its instruments. This joining either necessitates constant knowledge, or is not at all susceptible to knowledge. But neither of these two cases is true.[99]

Having determined that the rational soul intellects in itself and independently of the body, Ibn Sina returns to the issue of what happens to the soul after it separates from the body. He argues that the intelligibles that the soul acquires, and that are its essential perfections, are in themselves unchangeable and eternal. Therefore, the soul's acquisition of its essential perfections ensures its eternity after it leaves the body. In other words, once the soul attains its proper objects, which are eternal in themselves, it attains its actual eternity through them. Being a fundamental principle itself, the rational soul is simple and cannot be subject to composition of what is corruptible and what is incorruptible. Therefore its incorruptible essential perfections actualize and sustain its incorruptibility, which is the only thing possible for it.

In chapters 7 to 12 Ibn Sina first criticizes the ancient view, which he attributes to the Peripatetics and holds that for the rational soul to know or grasp intelligibles is for it to become one with its intelligibles. In al-Ishārāt, he does not expound this view and the proponents' arguments for it, but in al-Mabda' wal-Ma'ād he does.[100] But there he does not criticize it at all, and the reader may take it to be his own view. However, in his introduction to that work he asserts that his objective is to "show the views held by the Peripatetic scholars . . . to clarify in these essays what these scholars kept hidden, to declare what they left concealed and unstated, to collect what they dispersed, and to detail as much as possible what they left general."[101]

In *al-Ishārāt* he simply argues that this ancient view is untenable, classifying Porphyry's thoughts on the intellect and intelligibles as "bad ideas." He adds that, though they praise Porphyry's work on this subject, the Peripatetics do not understand the work, nor does he understand it either.

Ibn Sina's argument against this ancient view is along the following lines. If the view under consideration were true, when a soul knows a multiplicity of intelligibles, for example, it and every one of these intelligibles become one. Therefore, every one of this multiplicity of known objects becomes one with every other one. Thus, a multiplicity of known objects is also reduced to one thing, which cannot be the case. Also, if this view were true, then for X to know, for example, beauty at a certain time is to become beauty. However, for X to know ugliness at the same time is also to become ugliness. So the same knower would become two contradictory things simultaneously, which is impossible.

Ibn Sina then introduces his concept of what it is to know or to grasp intelligibles. For the soul to know a thing, he says, is for that thing to be represented, imprinted, or established in the existing essence or intellect of the soul as a thing is established in another. "Thus, it becomes apparent to you from this that whatever knows [anything] is an existing essence in which the intelligibles are established in the manner in which a thing is established in another."[102]

Now that the concept of knowledge is established, Ibn Sina moves on to determine the type of knowledge that is necessary in itself, the First, and the principles that follow it enjoy. After asserting that knowledge is the establishment of intelligibles in the existing essence or intellect of a thing, Ibn Sina recognizes that there are two ways in which this may happen. (1) Intelligibles may be established in an intellect after they are derived from external individual beings. This is exemplified in having the representation of chairness in the human intellect after deriving it from external individual chairs. (2) Intelligibles may also be established in an intellect prior to their external existence. An example is having the concept of a triangle prior to bringing it out externally and giving it concrete existence. Intelligibles of the first type are effects of external causes; while intelligibles of the second type are causes of external effects. That which is necessary in itself knows the whole in the second manner.

Each of the types of representations of intelligibles may be due to an external intellectual cause. It may also be due to an intellect itself, not to any external cause. "Were it not for this, there would be an infinity of separate intellects."[103] Representations of intelligibles due to an intellect itself must, therefore, belong to that which is necessary in itself.

It follows that that which is necessary in itself knows itself by itself and not due to any external being. However, it knows what follows from it inasmuch as it is the cause of the existence of those things. This is because for a thing to have complete knowledge of itself, as does the First, is to have knowledge of its effects. The First also knows the remaining things inasmuch as they are necessitated in the chain of things that flow from it in every way. Hence that which is necessary in itself knows all things.

Not only does that which is necessary in itself know all things, but it also knows them in its essence and by its essence, the highest and best essence. Therefore, its knowledge of things is the best manner in which a being may know, and the things it knows are the best known objects. Next to this highest and best manner of knowledge comes that of the intellectual principles or celestial intelligences. This is because they also know the First and what proceeds from it, but only through its illumination on them. The "impressions and sketches" that are imprinted on the rational souls—be they celestial or human—are last on the scale of epistemological value.

Ibn Sina is aware that the opponent may now raise the following objection. If, as claimed earlier, the intelligibles do not unite with the intellect that intellects them or with each other, but are different forms that are established in that intellect, and if that which is necessary in itself intellects everything, it follows that the various intelligibles in its essence cause a multiplicity in it.

He responds by reminding the opponent that since that which is necessary in itself knows its essence by its essence, and since its essence is the cause of multiplicity, it follows that it necessarily knows multiplicity by virtue of knowing its essence as the cause of multiplicity. In other words, the First knows itself independently as the cause of its effects or necessary concomitants to which multiplicity belongs.[104] This means that multiplicity is a necessary effect of the First, and, as such, it is posterior to it, not a constituent of it. As for why the First has different names when it is one, here is Ibn Sina's explanation: "A multiplicity of relative and non-relative concomitants as well as a multiplicity of negations occur to the First. This causes a multiplicity of names [for Him], but it does not affect the unity of His essence."[105]

Ibn Sina now turns his attention to the issue of the First's knowledge of particular things, which are by nature changeable. Particular things, he says, may be known in one of two ways: in a universal way or in a particular way. By the former is meant knowledge of things as necessitated by their causes or species, which are eternal universal natures contrary to the individuals that are subsumed under them; whereas by the latter is meant knowledge of particular things in time. That is why the former type of knowledge is eternal; while the latter changes with the changing of the particular things. An example of the former type is the intellect's grasping that an eclipse occurs when the moon is in such and such a state. This does not mean that the intellect knows that an eclipse has occurred, is occurring, or will occur at such and such a time. The latter type is exemplified by the intellect's grasping that an eclipse occurred yesterday at such and such a time.

Because the First's nature is eternal and not subject to any change, it cannot know particulars in a particular way. But it can and does know them in a universal way. This view was later challenged by al-Ghazali,[106] who viewed it as compromising the traditional Islamic view that God knows everything and that there is no atom on earth or in the heavens that escapes his knowledge.[107]

In addressing the issue of attributes by way of trying to show that the Divine attributes do not cause any change in the First's essence, Ibn Sina distinguishes between two main types of attributes: those that cause change in the essence of another thing if they undergo change and those that do not. In this work he gives the following example of the first type: when white becomes black, owing to "the change of a non-relative, fixed attribute."[108] Another example is the case when an intellect knows that a certain thing does not exist, but later that thing begins to exist. The intellect then knows that that thing exists. "Hence, the relation and the relative attribute change together" (292). The second type of attributes may be illustrated thus: When, for example, X has the power to move Y, but if Y ceases to exist, then X no longer has the power to move Y. However, though X no longer has its attribute (actual ability to move Y externally), still, its loss of this attribute does not cause any change in its essence, but only in its external particular relation. X's internal power to move Y, Ibn Sina would say, is in itself indivisible, but consequent upon it in a primary and an essential mode are attributes or relations to universal things. Also subsumed under such universals are particulars to which the same attribute or relation applies, yet in a secondary and an accidental mode.

> Its having power is an attribute of it which is one, and which is followed in a primary and an essential manner by a relation to a universal thing, such as moving bodies in a certain state, for example. Zayd, Amr, stone, and tree are also included in this [relation] but in a secondary [and accidental] manner. Its having power is not dependent on the individual relations in some unavoidable manner. If Zayd were not at all in possibility, and the relation of power to move him did not occur at all, this

would not harm [the mover's] power to move [things]. Thus, [the mover's] primary possession of power is not changed by the change of the states of that which is one of the things over which the power is exercised. Rather, it is just the external relations that change only.   (290–92)

In other words, an attribute that has a relation to universal things does not undergo any change, because universals do not change. Also, it cannot be affected by any change that individuals under universals undergo, because this attribute has no direct relation to these individuals but only one through intermediaries. Thus the change of individuals to which it has an intermediary relation is accidental to it.

Ibn Sina sums up his discussion of attributes by calling attention to the principle that a thing not subject to change cannot have attributes that undergo any change unless it is a distant change of particulars that relate to the attribute indirectly and therefore accidentally. Thus such change has no impact on the essence of the thing to which the attribute belongs. God is said not to be subject to change. Therefore his attributes, which are essential to him and apart from any relations, as well as those that have relations to universals, are unaffected by any change, and so is his essence. The change that belongs to members of universals is accidental to him, as it is accidentally related to him through the intermediary connection of their universals.

Ibn Sina closes the discussion of God's knowledge by recapitulating his view on the manner and extent of this knowledge. Thus he reiterates the idea that God's knowledge of particulars is universal and nontemporal. This means it does not include specific times, but is above any duration in time. If, for example, it included reference to past, present, or future times, it would undergo change, and, being an established or essential attribute of God, its change would cause change in him. Ibn Sina insists that this type of universal and nontemporal divine knowledge does not mean that God does not know everything. Rather, he knows everything inasmuch as everything is a necessary consequence of his essence whether through mediation or without mediation, and he knows his essence. Ibn Sina calls the detailing of the determined things in his essence through necessary existing manifestations of such things "destiny," without which nothing outside God can exist. "His destiny, which is the detailing of His first determination, leads in a necessary manner to [the existence of] everything individually, since as you have learned, that which is not necessitated is not" (297). In other words, for anything other than God to exist is to be destined by God to flow from him necessarily.

The remaining five chapters of the *Metaphysics* (chapters 22 to 27) are devoted to a study of providence, good, evil, and destiny. The ideas proposed in these chapters and similar ones in Ibn Sina's other works include a clear attempt to offer a theodicy in general and a solution to the problem of destiny in particular.

Ibn Sina begins with a discussion of providence, which he identifies as God's knowledge of the whole, of the manner necessary for the existence of the whole in the best order, and of the fact that the whole with its details necessarily flows from him by virtue of his knowledge of the whole. Thus existing things in the universe correspond to objects in his knowledge (297–99), but not by way of any intention on his part. Rather, the world is strictly a necessary cosmic system that takes on an existential nature outside his knowledge. That is to say, his knowledge of the best order is the source of the existence of the best order, including good and evil in it.

Ibn Sina acknowledges that the view of providence he adopts here and in many of his other writings[109] is in agreement with the one he attributes to his predecessors in *al-Mabda' wal-Ma'ād*. In that work, he says that by "providence" his predecessors meant "the prior knowledge that God, the exalted, has of the manner in which the whole of existence is possible, and of every part of it, its action and reaction, [as represented] in his essence. . . . [Providence is also his knowledge of] the manner in which the good emanates from him, as it is a consequence of his goodness, not that he intends it essentially. God, the exalted is not in need of anything else."[110]

Having established that all things were in God's knowledge prior to existing, Ibn Sina finds it necessary now to explain the existence of evil in a world that overflows from God, the pure good.[111]

Al-Ishārāt divides things in possibility into the following four types: (1) those that are good and free from evil, (2) those that cannot be good and beneficial without resulting in some evil at the jamming and clashing of things, (3) those that are absolutely evil, and (4) those that are evil for the most part.[112]

The first type is exemplified by the celestial intelligences, and the second by fire, which cannot be itself with all its benefits without at the same time having the capacity to burn and be destructive if it is in contact with combustible objects. The first type necessarily comes into existence as it emanates from the pure good. This type is found in the celestial sphere. The second type must also exist, as its goodness outweighs the accidental evil it causes. If its existence is eliminated by trying to eliminate a slight evil, more evil would be created. "This is because in the non-existence of much good and in the non-production of it, as a precaution against [the presence of] slight evil, there is great evil."[113] The second kind of evil is found in our world, the sublunary sphere.

As for the third and fourth types, nothing is said about their existence or nonexistence in *al-Ishārāt*, and no example of them is given. I assume that this is because, according to Ibn Sina, neither kind can exist. The reason (3) cannot exist is that the existence of a thing that is absolutely evil or a complete privation is a contradiction in terms. To be completely consumed by evil is to be nonexistent. Thus, since absolute evil or absolute privation has no real existence or being, and since existence or being is identified with goodness,[114] there is nothing good about absolute evil "except about the utterance of it."[115] Type (4), too, cannot exist. Ibn Sina does not offer anywhere a clear argument in support of this claim, but it seems that his thinking is along the following lines: A thing ceases to be what it is, in other words, ceases to exist as it is, if more than 50 percent of it is consumed by evil and becomes nonbeing.[116]

These four types of things listed in *al-Ishārāt* as in possibility are listed in *al-Shifā'* as five types of things in imagination. Here is how the text of *al-Shifā'* reads:

> Rather, we say that things in imagination are, if imagined as existing, either: (a) things which cannot but be absolutely evil; (b) things whose existence is good—it being impossible for them to be evil and deficient; (c) things in which goodness predominates, if their existence comes about—anything other than this is impossible for their nature; (d) things in which evilness predominates; and (e) things in which the two states [goodness and evilness] are equal.
>
> As for that in which there is no evilness, it exists in the nature [of things]. Regarding that which is completely evil, or that [in which evil] predominates, or also that [in which evil] equals [the good, these] do not exist. However, that in whose existence the good predominates it is more suitable that it exists—if what is predominate in it is its being good.[117]

The preceding analysis of the types of evil leaves us with the following curious questions. If (3) and (4) listed in *al-Ishārāt* or (a) and (d) plus (e) listed in *al-Shifā'* cannot exist under any circumstance, why are they included among things possible in existence or things imagined as existing? Is it possible, for example, for absolute evil to be among the things possible in existence or imagined as existing, when by definition absolute evil is empty of and negates any degree of existence?

Ibn Sina's theodicy echoes the Platonic and Aristotelian arguments for "the higher good defense," which holds that every part of the universe and every action taken is for the purpose of the whole: "If there is nothing other than the person afflicted by destiny, there would not be much general and universal utility in his particular corruption. For the sake of the universal, attention should not be paid from the point of view of the particular. Similarly, for the sake of the whole, attention should not be paid from the point of view of the part. Thus, an organ that hurts is severed in order that the body as a whole be saved."[118]

Here is what Plato says in this regard:

> He who provides for the world has disposed all things with a view to the preservation and perfection of the whole, wherefore each several thing, also, so far as may be, does and has done to it what is meet. And for each and all there are, in every case, governors appointed of all doing and being-done-to, down to the least detail, who have achieved perfection even to the minute particulars. Thine own being, also, fond man, is one such fragment, and so, for all its littleness, all its striving is ever directed toward the whole, but thou has forgotten in the business that the purpose of all that happens is what we have said, to win bliss for the life of the whole; it is not made for thee, but thou for it.[119]

Aristotle's thought also goes like this: "And all things are ordered together somehow, but not all alike—both fishes and fowls and plants; and the world is not such that one thing has nothing to do with another, but they are connected. For they all are ordered together to one end . . . and there are functions similarly in which all share for the good of the whole."[120]

In any case, Ibn Sina believes that despite the presence of evil, this is the best of all possible worlds, as Leibniz after him,[121] among others, asserts. Besides, evil in the world is limited to the sublunary sphere and is rare in comparison with the good. Additionally, individuals who suffer evil in this world are fewer in number than those who do not suffer it. The idea of the rarity of "real" evil is elaborated in al-Shifā', al-Ilāhiyyāt as follows: "All causes of evil are only found in the sublunary world. And the whole of the sublunary world is small in relation to the rest of existence, as you have learned. Furthermore, evil only strikes individuals, and at certain time. The species, [on the other hand,] are preserved. Except for one kind of evil [the accidental one] real evil does not extend to a majority of individuals."[122]

In other words, the claim here is that the type of evil that is rare is only real or essential evil. This type of evil is called "essential" not because it belongs to the essence or nature of a thing, but because it is the removal of one or more aspects or "fixed perfections" of the essence or nature of a thing.[123] Ibn Sina grants, however, that accidental evil is predominant. This type of evil could be (1) "non-existent" (that is, a privation, but of an accident of a thing—an accident of a thing is something whose removal does not affect the essence or nature of that thing); (2) a "destroyer"; or (3) something "which withholds perfection from what deserves it."[124]

An example of essential evil is blindness in the human eye. An example of essential evil from one point of view and accidental evil from another point of view is the high mountains and clouds that prevent sunlight from reaching a plant that needs sunlight for its growth.[125] While the plant's loss of growth is essential evil for the plant, it is accidental evil for the mountains and clouds. Fire burning a monk's garment, for example, is accidental evil for both the fire and the monk.

The *Metaphysics* concludes with an attempt to address the problem of destiny, which is a particular form of the problem of evil. The former problem is posed by this question: If there is destiny, why is there reward and punishment? This is assuming that God is just. (As mentioned earlier, by "destiny" is meant the detailing of the determined things in God's essence from which things necessarily flow and come to exist.) The latter is a more general problem, which in its traditional form asserts the following: If God exists, if He is all-knowing, all-powerful, and all-good, why does He cause or allow evil?

Ibn Sina responds to the first problem by defining "reward" and "punishment" in a nontraditional way.[126] He asserts, as does Ibn Rushd after him,[127] that reward and punishment are necessary consequences of the human conditions in this life: "Punishment of the soul for its

sin is, as you shall know, similar to the disease of the body for its gluttony. Thus, it is one of the necessary consequences to which past
conditions lead—these conditions together with their consequences
are inescapable."[128]

What about "reward" and "punishment" in the sense related by
the prophets? Ibn Sina seems convinced that this type of reward and
punishment is not real. Still, it acts as an incentive for individuals to
desire the former and try to seek it by acting rightly, and to fear the
latter and try to restrain themselves from performing bad actions.
Of course, the effort to seek to act rightly and restrain oneself from
doing bad actions serves the general good of society. In this the idea
of an external dispenser of reward and punishment is beneficial. Sin-
gling out punishment to illustrate his point, Ibn Sina says, "As for the
punishment that falls in another class, which has its principle from
without, that is another story. Further, if a punisher from without is
accepted, that is also good. This is because it is necessary that fear be
present among the causes that are confirmed and, hence, useful in
general. Belief [in such punishment] ensures fear."[129]

In short, rewards and punishments are not handed out by God.
Rather, they are mere consequences of our past conditions. Thus,
according to Ibn Sina, there is no inconsistency between the following two propositions: "We are destined" and "we are rewarded and
punished." This is because while destiny is attributed to God, rewards
and punishments are not.

However, one cannot help but ask whether God is not also the
cause of rewards and punishments, though in an indirect way or
through mediation. Without being first destined or determined in
God's essence, things cannot exist externally, according to Ibn Sina.
If so, the past conditions that necessarily result in rewards or punishments must have been first destined or determined in God's essence,
from which they proceeded to external existence. In other words,
everything that exists, including past human conditions, proceeds to
existence from God. The past human conditions necessarily lead to
rewards or punishments. Therefore, through the mediation of these

conditions, rewards and punishments may be said to proceed from God.

Ibn Sina's response to the problem of evil is discussed and elaborated in my work *The Problem of Evil: Ibn Sina's Theodicy*. For the present purposes, one may summarize the theses he introduces in response to the problem as follows:

1. God is absolutely good, and, because of his goodness, he does not lack anything. Because he is fully sufficient, he cannot intend any good or evil in the world. The contention is that one intends to fulfill what one lacks.
2. God is providential, and everything in existence overflows from him as a result of his providence. Evil simply overflows from God as a feature of the universe that overflows from God.
3. There is more good than evil in the universe. Essential or real evil is only in the sublunary sphere, where it is also rare and affects a minority of individuals. Nonessential or accidental evil, on the other hand, is predominant.
4. Evil is a necessary consequence of the good, and to wish the removal of evil is to wish the removal of the good.
5. Evil is a necessary means for the good.
6. God is not omnipotent in the traditional sense, but only in the sense of having the power to fulfill all possibilities. Thus, God cannot free the world from evil, which is part of its possibilities and nature. Therefore, as Plato and Plotinus taught, evil is ineradicable.[130]
7. Essential evil is privation of being and therefore cannot be caused by God, who is the cause of being only.
8. Human evil is due to the human free will.

Of course, Ibn Sina's response to the problems of destiny and of evil is unsatisfactory from an Islamic point of view. The denial of the traditional concepts of reward and punishment and the limitation of

God's omnipotence to the ability to fulfill whatever is possible are but two clear examples of ideas unacceptable to Islam, despite Ibn Sina's use of such Islamic terminology as *reward, punishment,* and *omnipotence.*

The *Physics* and *Metaphysics* portray Ibn Sina's universe with its celestial and terestial spheres, its primary and secondary principles, and its purpose of seeking its perfection. The fourth part of *al-Ishārāt, Mysticism,* focuses particularly on the purpose of being human, the manner in which this purpose may be achieved, and the outcome of achieving it or falling short of doing so. Thus, the *Metaphysics,* which is primarily an inquiry into existence, with special emphasis on God and his relation to the rest of existence and on the hierarchy of metaphysical value built in this cosmic system, is intended to constitute a link between the study of nature and that of the rational human soul to serve as guidance to achieve the proper human ends of eternity and happiness and to avoid their contraries.

PART TWO
Physics

[Prologue] (p. 147)

In the name of God, the Compassionate, the Merciful!

These are remarks concerning principles and admonitions concerning fundamentals. He whose way is made easy will be enlightened by them, but he whose way is made difficult will not benefit [even] from what is clearer than they are. Now we rely on [God's] guidance.

Once again, I state my wish and repeat my request for high frugality in giving away the contents of these parts to anyone who does not meet the conditions that I posit at the end of these remarks.

FIRST CLASS (P. 149)

On the Substance of Bodies

CHAPTER 1. DELUSION AND REMARK:
ON THE COMPOSITION OF BODIES (P. 152)

Some people believe that every body has joints that hold together parts which are not bodies, but of which bodies are composed. They also claim that such parts are not receptive to division either by fracture, by cutting, by imagination, or by hypothesis, and that those parts of them falling in the middle of the organization prevent the two extremes from contact [with each other] (p. 153).[1]

They do not know that if the middle [part] is such, each of the two extremes receives (p. 154) from it something other than that which is received by the other, and that neither of them receives the middle part as a whole. If one allows that any of the two extremes merges with the center, so that there will be one thing in their place or space—or call it what you please—that extreme cannot but penetrate the center (p. 155); thus encountering what it had not encountered [prior to the penetration]. The quantity it had received is other than [that which it receives at] the assumed encounter of the merge (p. 156). The assumed encounter of the merge necessitates that that which encounters the center also encounters the other extreme, as the center encounters it, and that it not be distinguished in position [from the other extreme] (p. 157), since there is no void at its encounter [with it]. At that point there is no organization, no middle part, no extreme, and no increase in volume. If any of this were to occur, none of what happens when encountering the whole in the assumed merge will occur. Rather, there will be void and that which is encountered will be divided (p. 158).[2]

Chapter 2. Delusion and Remark: Another Theory Concerning the Composition of Bodies of Infinite Parts

Some other people[3] speak of almost this kind of composition,[4] but which is of infinite parts (p. 159).

They do not know that every multiplicity, be it finite or infinite, includes both the one and the finite. If every finite included in the multiplicity is composed of units whose volume is not (p. 160) greater than that of the one, then the composition of the units does not increase in quantity, but perhaps does so in number.

If a finite multiplicity is of units whose volume is greater than that of the one (p. 161), and among which relations are possible in all directions so that there is volume in every direction, then there will be a body. The relation of the volume of this body to the volume of that whose units are infinite (p. 162) is the same as the relation of that whose quantity is finite to that whose quantity is finite. But increase in volume is in accordance with increase in composition and order. Thus the relation of the finite units to those that are infinite will be the same as the relation of the finite to the finite. But this is absurd and impossible.

CHAPTER 3. ADMONITION: EVIDENCE FOR THE UNSOUNDNESS OF THE ABOVE THEORIES (P. 163)

Is it not the case that if consideration requires that a body cannot be composed of infinite joined parts, and that it is not necessary that every (p. 164) body has indivisible, finite joined parts, then it must be the case that the existence of a body whose extension does not possess joined parts is possible (p. 165)? Rather, it is in itself as it is to the senses.[5] However, it is not one of those things that are indivisible in every way. On the contrary, it must have the capacity for division.

The joined parts are produced either by disjunction, by cutting, by diversity of two fixed accidents—as in something spotted with two different colors—by imagination or by hypothesis,[6] if disjunction is prevented for some reason.

CHAPTER 4. A FOLLOW-UP: ON THE INFINITY OF THE IMAGINATIVE DIVISION OF BODIES (P. 166)

Is it not the case that if a composition is not of units that do not accept division, then one of the manners of this division, especially that of the imagination, must go on to infinity? This is a matter on which scholars have placed great emphasis. He who is endowed with insight will be guided by the material we present.

CHAPTER 5. ADMONITION: REGARDING MOVEMENT AND TIME AS ALSO DIVISIBLE TO INFINITY (P. 167)

You shall also know from what you have already learned concerning the capacity of measures for division to infinity that movement and the time of this movement are also such[7] and that, again, neither movement nor time is composed of indivisible [parts].

Chapter 6. Remark: Regarding the Difference Between That Which Is Continuous in Itself and That Which Has the Capacity for Continuity (p. 168)

You have already learned that a body has a continuous firm quantity (p. 170) and that division and disjunction may occur to it.[8] You [also] know that that which is continuous in itself[9] is other than that which has the capacity for receiving continuity and division, in a manner which is itself described by continuity and division (p. 171). Thus, the capacity for this reception is other than being actually receptive and other than its disposition and form (p. 172). Such a capacity belongs to something other than the essence of that which is continuous in itself, which (p. 173), if divided, is annihilated and something else comes into being. But if continuity is brought back, something like it comes into being once again.

Chapter 7. Delusion and Admonition: Concerning the Unity of the Nature of Corporeal Extension in Itself (p. 174)

Perhaps you will say that if this is necessitated, it is so only in the case of that which accepts disjunction and disintegration. And I do not think that every body is such.[10]

If you think so, you must know that the nature of corporeal extension is in itself one and the same (p. 175) and cannot dispense with the receptacle or the need for the receptacle. If its need for that in which it subsists is known in some of its states, then it is known that its nature cannot dispense with that in which it subsists. If its nature were of the kind that subsists by itself, wherever it has an essence, it has this nature. This is because it is a realized specific nature, differing in external qualities (p. 176) and not in specific differences.

CHAPTER 8. DELUSION AND ADMONITION: CONCERNING THE WAYS IN WHICH DISJUNCTION IS POSSIBLE FOR THAT WHICH IS CONTINUOUS (P. 177)

Or perhaps you will say that the one corporeal extension is not receptive to division at all and that the only body that divides is that which is composed of simple bodies (p. 178) having no capacity for division except that which occurs in accordance with hypothesis, imagination, or the like.

If you think so, you must know that division by imagination (p. 179), by hypothesis, or by that which occurs due to the diversity of two fixed accidents, as white and black in a variegated thing, or by two relatives, as the diversity of two opposite or parallel elements or two adjacent ones creates in the divided thing a certain duality in which the nature of each of the two has the nature of the other, the nature of the whole, and the nature of an external thing pertaining to the same species (p. 180).[11] What is true of every two of them is true of any other two. Thus continuity that eliminates duality and disjunction and is true of two continuous elements is also true of two divergent ones. Similarly, disjunction, which eliminates continuous unity and is true of two divergent elements, is also true of two continuous ones, except if something external to the nature of the extension—be that a necessary concomitant or a perishable one—obstructs and prevents [this]. Perhaps if this obstacle were a natural necessary concomitant, then there would be no actual duality (p. 181) and no division among the individuals of the species of that nature. Rather, its species would be in its individual.

CHAPTER 9. ADMONITION: CONCERNING WHY A SPECIES FOR WHICH IT IS POSSIBLE TO HAVE A PLURALITY OF INDIVIDUALS MAY BE OBSTRUCTED FROM HAVING MORE THAN ONE

The possible individuals of any species that is capable of having a plurality of individuals and that is obstructed from having that by a natural necessary obstacle will not be (p. 182) subject to any duality or plurality. Rather, its kind is in its individual; that is, there is only one individual of this species. How could a duality or a plurality belong to the individuals of that species when the obstacle to this is a natural necessary concomitant?

CHAPTER 10. A FOLLOW-UP: CONCERNING THE FIRST MATTER AS THAT WHICH IN ITSELF HAS NO QUANTITY AND IN WHICH ANY QUANTITY CAN SUBSIST

Has it not become evident to you that the quantity, inasmuch as it is a quantity, or the corporeal form, inasmuch as it is a corporeal form, is linked to the thing (p. 183) in which it subsists and in which it is a form? That thing is its matter and something which in itself is neither a quantity nor a corporeal form of it. This is the first matter which you must therefore know.

Do not think it is far-fetched that the reception of a determined quantity, to the exclusion of what is smaller or larger than it, is not specified in certain things.

CHAPTER 11. REMARK: CONCERNING THE EVIDENCE FOR THE FINITUDE OF DISTANCES

You must realize that if it were possible for a distance to extend in a plenum or in a void, it could not go on to infinity (p. 185); otherwise it would be possible to assume two infinite lines branching out of the same point, with the distance between them never ceasing to increase. It would be possible also to assume distances between them increasing to the same degree. Again, it would be possible to assume these distances between them as going on to infinity (p. 186). Thus, there would be the possibility of an increase to infinity over the gap that was first assumed, because any increase there is, together with what is increased upon, may be present in one distance. If there is any possible increase, then it is possible to have a distance that (p. 187) includes all this possible [increase]; otherwise, it is possible to have distances leading to a limit upon which it is not possible to make an increase (p. 188). Thus it would be possible to have only that which includes the limited in the group of the potentially unlimited. Hence the distance between the two lines becomes confined in its increase to a limit that does not surpass it in greatness. It is unavoidable that the two lines end there and do not penetrate beyond this limit; otherwise there may be increase beyond what is possible, i.e., beyond this limited thing in the group of the unlimited things. But this is impossible (p. 189).

Therefore it is evident that there is here the possibility of a distance between the first two lines (p. 190) that has those increases that go on to infinity. Thus the unlimited is confined between two delimitants. But this is impossible. You may also draw evidence for the impossibility of this in other ways in which one may resort or not resort to movement. But what we have already mentioned is sufficient.

Chapter 12. Remark: Concerning the Necessary Accompaniment of Shape to Corporeal Extension (p. 191)

It has already become clear to you that corporeal extension must be accompanied by finitude. Thus it must be accompanied by shape; I mean in existence (p. 192).[12]

Shape necessarily accompanies the corporeal extension [in one of three ways]: [1] Shape necessarily accompanies the corporeal extension, if, due to itself, the latter is isolated in itself.[13] [2] Shape follows the corporeal extension and necessarily accompanies it, if the latter is isolated in itself due to an efficient cause that has influence upon it. Or [3] shape necessarily accompanies the corporeal extension due to the subject and the things that contain the subject.[14]

If shape necessarily accompanies the corporeal extension, [when, due to itself, the latter] is isolated in itself, then bodies become similar

(p. 193) in the measures of extensions and in the dispositions of limits and shapes. Further, the supposed part of a certain measure would be necessarily accompanied by what necessarily accompanies the whole of that measure.

If shape necessarily accompanies the corporeal extension due to an efficient cause that exerts influence (p. 194), [when] the corporeal extension is isolated in itself, then, without (p. 195) its matter, the corporeal measure is receptive in itself to disjunction and conjunction and has in itself the capacity for reaction. But the impossibility of this has already been made clear.

It remains, therefore, that this occurs in association with the subject.[15]

CHAPTER 13. DELUSION AND REMARK: CONCERNING THE CAUSE OF THE SHAPE OF THE SPHERE

Perhaps you may say that this too will follow in other things—the supposed part of a sphere does not have the shape of a sphere (p. 196). Then you add that the shape of a sphere requires the nature of the sphere and that the nature of the part and the nature of the whole are one.

We say to you (p. 197) that shape occurs to the sphere from the nature of a force[16] that requires this [kind of] corporeality[17] for the matter of the sphere and does not require this corporeality for it from the matter itself (p. 198) or from the corporeality of the matter. Since this was required for the matter of the sphere, the necessity of this cause required that that which is assumed posterior to this be a part and does not have what belongs to the whole. This is because it was assumed to be a part posterior to the coming into being of the form of the whole. This occurs to the whole due to an accident[18] and an obstacle[19] and is caused by the association with that which is receptive to that form, supports it, and is differentiated by it.[20]

As for the measure, if it were isolated, and if there were nothing that necessitates (p. 199) something other than the nature of measurement—this nature being in itself one—this nature would not become a whole or something other than a whole, in accordance with this assumption, either by itself or by an [external] cause or by association with a receptive element.

Thus this nature does not merit a specific thing with diversity, even [if it were] universality itself or particularity. Therefore it is not possible to say here that something follows this nature due to something other than itself in a prior manner, in accordance with a certain possibility or potentiality, or in accordance with the propriety of the subject. This then is followed by the becoming of what is a part in a state different [from that of the whole].

CHAPTER 14. ADMONITION: CONCERNING THE CAUSE OF POSITION (P. 200)

This subject[21] has position[22] only due to the association of the corporeal form with it (p. 201). If it were to have position in the definition of its essence, when it is divided, then it will have volume in the definition of its essence. And, when it is not divided, then it will have in its definition the cutting of a limit to which one can point, [either as] a point, if it were not divided at all, or [as] a line or plain, if it were divided in a direction other than that to which one can point.[23]

CHAPTER 15. ADMONITION: CONCERNING THE NECESSITY OF FORM FOR POSITION (P. 202)

If we suppose a matter without form, it is without position. [If] it is then followed by a form and acquires a specific position (p. 203), it cannot be said that this [specific position] occurs because the form follows it there, as it can be said if it were to have a form that necessitates for it a position there or if a position there had occurred to it and then (p. 204) it was followed by the other form.

But this is not possible in [the case] under consideration, because matter is free from [form] according to this supposition. Nor is it possible to say also that the form has determined (p. 205) for this matter a specific position which is one of the particular positions that belong, for example, to the parts of every individual [element] such as the parts of earth; as it can be said in the case we had mentioned that a particular position is specified due to the following of the form.

There is a particular position that follows in a manner that specifies the nearest natural position to that position. An example of this is a part of air that becomes water. Its natural position is specified due to its first position, which is a closer natural place to water than that which has been a place for what has become water, that is, air. Nor is this possible only because we are supposing matter to be free from [form].

CHAPTER 16. A FOLLOW-UP: CONCLUSION REGARDING THE NECESSITY OF CORPOREAL FORM FOR MATTER (P. 207)

Derive from this that matter is not free from corporeal form.

CHAPTER 17. ADMONITION: CONCERNING MATTER AS ALSO NOT FREE FROM FORMS OTHER THAN CORPOREAL ONES (P. 208)

Matter may also not be free from other forms. How [could it be so free, when bodies] must be either [1] with a form that necessitates the easy reception of disjunction, conjunction, and figuration, [2 with a form that necessitates this reception] with difficulty, or [3] with (p. 209) a form that necessitates the prevention of this reception. But none of this is required by corporeality. Again, [a body] necessarily merits a determined proper place or a determined proper position (p. 210). None of this is required by the general corporeality (p. 211) common to [bodies].

CHAPTER 18. REMARK: CONCERNING THE FACT THAT, IN ADDITION TO MATTER, THERE IS NECESSITY FOR EXTERNAL DETERMINANTS OF THE CORPOREAL FORM (P. 212)

You must know that the existence of the subject[24] is also not sufficient for determining a corporeal form. If it were, the already-mentioned similitude [in quantity and shape] would be necessary.[25] Rather (p. 213), that whose states are different requires external determinants and states that work together in harmony to determine the required quantity and shape.[26] This is a secret that will help you understand other secrets.[27]

CHAPTER 19. DELUSION AND ADMONITION: ON THE JOINING OF MATTER AND FORM AS NECESSARY FOR THE ACTUAL SUBSISTENCE OF MATTER (P. 214)

You must know that in order for matter to have actual subsistence it must be joined to the form.[28] Thus either [1] The form is the primary and unrestricted cause (p. 215) of the matter's subsistence.[29] [2] The form is an instrument or an intermediary (p. 216) for something else that employs it without restriction to make matter subsist by itself. [3] The form is a partner with something else; on the basis of the union of both, matter subsists (p. 217). Or [4] Matter is not free from form, nor form from matter; neither of them is better fit than the other to make the other subsist (p. 218). Rather, there is a certain cause external to them that makes each of them subsist with the other and by the other.

CHAPTER 20. REMARK: ON THE DEPARTURE OF FORMS FROM ONE MATTER TO ANOTHER

As for the forms that separate from one matter to another, one cannot say of them that they are either unrestricted causes of the one continuous existence (p. 219) of their matters or unrestricted instruments or intermediaries. Rather, such forms must fall in one of the two remaining divisions.[30] Here there is another secret.[31]

CHAPTER 21. REMARK: CONCERNING THE DEMONSTRATION THAT THE CORPOREAL FORMS CANNOT BE INDEPENDENT OR INTERMEDIARY CAUSES OF MATTER (P. 220)

You must know in brief that none of the corporeal forms (p. 221), or what accompanies them,[32] is an unrestricted cause of the subsistence of matter (p. 223). If they were unrestricted causes of the subsistence of matter, they would be prior to matter in existence, and the things that are causes of the quiddity of the form or of the form's being in positive existence[33] would also be prior to matter in existence; so that after this the existence of matter would be produced by the existence of the form (p. 224). The former, though, is an effect of a certain genus whose essence is inseparable from that of (p. 225) the cause, even though matter is not one of the states of the form that are effects of the form's quiddity; for (p. 226) the concomitant effects are of two types,[34] each of which exists (p. 227).

But it had been learned that corporeal form is not defined in itself except by or with, among other things, limit and shape.[35] It was also made evident that matter is a cause of both limit and shape.[36] Thus matter becomes one of the causes by which or with which the existence of the prior form is completed by the completion of the existence of the form for matter. This is impossible.[37]

Hence it has become clear that the form cannot be an unrestricted cause or an intermediary for matter.

CHAPTER 22. DELUSION AND ADMONITION: REFUTATION OF THE CLAIM THAT MATTER IS THE CAUSE OF THE EXISTENCE OF THE FORM (P. 228)

Perhaps you will say that if matter is needed in order for the form to have existence, then matter becomes a cause prior in existence to the form (p. 229).

The answer is that we have not required that matter is needed in order for the form to have existence. Rather, in brief, we have required that matter is needed for the existence of things[38] by which or with which the form exists. A capitulation of what follows requires a detailed discussion.

CHAPTER 23. REMARK: CONCERNING THE SUBSISTENCE OF MATTER DURING THE PROCESS OF FORM SUBSTITUTION

You know that if the corporeal form separates from matter (p. 230) and is not substituted [by another corporeal form], then matter ceases to exist. Thus that which makes the substitution inevitably makes matter subsist by virtue of the substitution. We must not say[39] that the substitute also subsists by virtue of matter (p. 231), since matter subsists and then makes [something else] subsist. This is because that which subsists and then makes [something else] subsist is prior in subsistence [to that thing] either in time or in essence. In short, you cannot make subsistence circular.

CHAPTER 24. REMARK: CONCERNING THE PRIORITY OF FORM TO MATTER (P. 232)

It is not possible to have two things, each of which makes the other subsist, so that each of which is prior in existence to the other and to itself. Nor is it permissible to have two things, each of which necessarily subsists simultaneously with the other (p. 233). This is because if the essence of each of them does not depend on the other,[40] then it is permissible for each of them to subsist by itself, even if it were without the other. If, on the other hand, the essence of each of them depends (p. 234) on the other, then the essence of each of them affects the completion of the existence of the other. But this is one of the things that have been shown to be impossible (p. 235).

Therefore it remains that the dependency is only one-sided. Thus matter and form are not of the same degree of dependency and simultaneity. Rather, the form has a certain priority in the generable and corruptible. Now, this priority must be investigated.

CHAPTER 25. REMARK: ON THE MANNER IN WHICH FORM IS PRIOR

This [priority] is only possible in one of the remaining divisions (p. 236).[41] That is, matter exists due to [1] a primary cause[42] and [2] a determinant of the succession of forms.[43] When these two things unite, the existence of matter is completed (p. 237). Then, by means of matter, the form is individuated and, by the form, the matter is also individuated (p. 238) in a manner whose evidence merits a discussion beyond this summary.

CHAPTER 26. DELUSION AND ADMONITION: CONCERNING THE PRIORITY IN ESSENCE OF THE CAUSE TO THE EFFECT DESPITE THE TEMPORAL SIMULTANEITY OF THE TWO (P. 239)

Perhaps you will say that since the removal of each of these two things removes the other, then each of them is the same as the other in priority and posteriority.

What can rid you of this [view] is a principle that you can determine. Here it is: the cause is like the movement of your hand with the key. If it is removed, the effect, such as the movement of the key, is also removed. But if the effect is removed, the cause is not also removed;

for the removal of the movement of the key is not what removes the movement of your hand, even though it is simultaneous with it. Rather, its removal is only possible since the cause, i.e., the movement of your hand, had already been removed (p. 240) The two—I mean the two removals—are simultaneous in time, but the removal of the cause is prior in essence to the removal of the effect, as is [the case] in their affirmation and their existence.

Chapter 27. A Follow-up: The Inference to Be Drawn Regarding the Similarity Between the Priority of the Form That Is Inseparable from Its Matter and of That Which Is Separable

You must discern by yourself and know that the case with regard to that whose form is inseparable from it is the same as this case in the priority of form.[44]

Chapter 28. Admonition: The Priority of the Body to the Surface, the Surface to the Line, and the Line to the Point (p. 241)

The body is limited by its simple element, [i.e., its surface] which is its section. Its simple element is limited by its line, which is its section (p. 242). And the line is limited by its point, which is its section (p. 243).

The body is necessarily accompanied by the surface, not inasmuch as its corporeality is constituted by the surface, but inasmuch as it is necessarily accompanied by limit after being a body (p. 244). Indeed, neither the body's possession of a surface nor its being limited is something that enters in its conception as a body. Because of this, it is possible for a certain group of people to conceive an unlimited body, until the impossibility of this thing that they conceive is made evident to them (p. 245).

As for the surface, such as the surface of a sphere without the consideration of movement or section, it is found without a line. But the axes, the two poles and the two circles, are among what occurs with movement.

The line, such as the circumference of a circle, may be found without a point (p. 246). Regarding the center, [it appears as a point] when diameters intersect, when there is a certain movement, or by hypothesis (p. 247). Before that the presence of a point in the middle is like the presence of a point in the two thirds and in other unlimited things. There is no center and there are no other joints of the parts of quantities except after the occurrence of movement or division that are not necessary [for the spheres].

If you hear [it said] in the definition of the circle that in its interiority there is a point, this means that it is possible to suppose a point in it. Similarly, it is said that the body is that which is divided into all dimensions. This means that it is possible to divide it into all dimensions.

You learn from this that in existence, the body is prior to the surface, the surface to the line, and the line to the point. This has already been determined by the scholars. When the converse of it is stated, namely that by its movement the point produces the line, then the line produces the surface, and, finally, the surface produces the body, it is [so stated to facilitate] understanding, conception, and imagination (p. 248). Do you not see that if the point is supposed as moving, then something in which it can move must also be supposed? This is a certain quantity: a line or a surface. So how could this be formed after its movement?

Chapter 29. Admonition: On the Absence of the Interpenetration of Corporeal Dimensions

It is so easy for you to be disposed to consider that the interpenetration of corporeal dimensions is prevented and that no body penetrates (p. 249) another body facing it and not removed from it. This is true of dimensions and not of matter, nor of the rest of the forms and accidents.

Chapter 30. Remark: Concerning Quantitative Distances Among Disjoined Bodies

You find that bodies in their positions are sometimes joined, sometimes close, and sometimes distant (p. 250). You may also find them in their positions such that [the space] between them is sometimes wide enough for bodies of fixed quantities, sometimes for greater quantities, and sometimes for smaller quantities.

It is clear that as bodies that are disjoined have different positions, they also have among them distances the estimation of which and of what falls in them is subject to variation—this variation being quantitative. Thus, if it were possible that such bodies have void among them and not bodies, then this void too will be an estimable distance. This void is not as some say "a pure nothing," even though it is not a body.

Chapter 31. Admonition: On the Nonexistence of Void

Since it has been shown that the continuous dimension is not constituted without matter, and that (p. 251) the corporeal dimensions do not interpenetrate due to their distances, then no void that is a pure distance exists.

If bodies begin their motions, then what is among them is displaced and no disrupted distance can be affirmed of them. Thus there is no void.

Chapter 32. Remark: On the Existence of Direction

It may befit what is under consideration to discuss the concept of (p. 252) what is called direction, exemplified in such statements as "Such a thing has moved in such a direction and not in another direction." It is known that if direction did not exist it would be impossible for the movable to seek it. How could one point toward nothing? It is evident, therefore, that direction exists.

Chapter 33. Remark: Direction Is of a Sensible, Not an Intelligible Nature

You must know that since direction is among the things toward which movement occurs, it is not one of the intelligibles that do not have position. Thus, due to its position, direction must be something toward which one can point ostensibly.

Chapter 34. Remark: Direction Is an Undivided Extremity of Dimension and Toward Which Movement Can Be Made (p. 253)

Since direction has position, it is clear that its position is in a dimension toward which pointing and movement are possible. If its position lies outside this dimension, then neither pointing nor movement toward it can be made (p. 254).

Further, this direction is either divided in that dimension or it is not. If it is divided, then, if the moving thing reaches one of its two parts assumed to be closer to the moving thing, yet did not stop, it is inevitable that it will be said either that it is still moving toward the direction or that it is moving away from it. If it is still moving toward the direction, then the direction is behind the divided. If, on the other hand, it is moving away from the direction, then what it has reached is the direction and not a part of it.

It is clear, therefore, that direction is an undivided limit in that dimension. It is an extremity of the dimension and a direction for the movement.

Thus you must now make an effort to know how the extremities of dimensions are determined by nature and what the reasons for this are. You must also know the states of the natural movements.

Chapter 35. Delusion and Admonition: Concerning the Concrete Existence of Direction as Opposed to Its Conceptual Being (p. 255)

You may say that it is not a condition of that toward which movement can be made that it exists.

A changeable thing may move from black to white, without white being in existence yet.[45] If you think so, then you must know that there is a difference between the two cases. Further, that concerning which you have expressed doubt does not occur in what we have in mind.

Regarding the difference, that which moves toward the direction does not make the direction among those things whose essence is expected to exist by the movement, but among those things whose essence is expected to be reached or approached by the movement. At the completion of the movement this difference does not give the direction a state of existence or of nonexistence that was not there at the time of the movement.[46]

As for the other [point], if the direction were such that it acquired existence by movement (p. 256), its existence would be the existence of something that has position and not a conceptual existence for which there is no position. It is this that we have in mind. The truth is that which [was pointed out in the discussion of] the difference on which what will follow this.

On the Directions and Their Primary and Secondary Bodies

CHAPTER 1. REMARK: CONCERNING THE DIRECTIONS THAT CHANGE AND THOSE THAT DO NOT

You must know that people point to directions that do not change, such as the directions of upward and downward (p. 258). They also point to directions that change by hypothesis, such as the right and the left of what surrounds us and what resembles them (p. 259).[1] Let us bypass what is by hypothesis.

As for what occurs by nature, it does not change in any manner.

CHAPTER 2. REMARK: CONCERNING THE DETERMINATION OF THE POSITION OF A DIRECTION (P. 260)

Further, it is impossible for the position of the direction to be determined in a void or in a uniform plenum.[2] A uniform thing has no limit that is more deserving than another of being a direction opposed to another direction. Therefore, the position of a direction must occur in something outside both of them.[3] It is necessary that this thing be either a body or bodily. A single delimitant, inasmuch as it is such, if supposed, one only supposes a single limit of it—this limit being what surrounds it.

In every dimension two directions occur; these are two extremities (p. 261). Since the directions that occur by nature are the upward and the downward—and these are two—it follows that either the delimitation occurs by a single body, not inasmuch as it is single, or it occurs by two bodies.

[In the case of] the delimitation by two bodies, it is either that one of these two bodies surrounds and the other is surrounded, or that the positions of the two bodies are apart (p. 262). If one of the two bodies surrounds and the other is surrounded, then the latter enters accidentally under the influence [of the other]. This is because that which surrounds alone determines the two extremities of the dimension, by the proximity that is determined by what surrounds it and by the distance that is determined by its center—whether there is void or plenum inside it or outside it.

If [the delimitation] occurs in the other manner, the direction of proximity is determined; but the direction of the distance must not be determined by [the body]. This is because distance from it must not be determined in a specific manner, unless [the body] is that which surrounds. Nor is the second [body] more fit than the first to be at a certain distance rather than at another possible distance, except due to [the interference of] an obstacle that necessarily helps in determining the direction and that is corporeal. But the discourse involved in its supposition and consideration of its position is circular.

Therefore it is evident that determining and fixing a direction is achieved by a single body only—not because this body has just any sort of nature—but inasmuch as (p. 263) it is in a certain state that necessitates the determination of two opposite [limits]. If the body is not one that surrounds, proximity is determined by it, but that which lies opposite it is not determined by it.

CHAPTER 3. REMARK: CONCERNING THE BODY THAT DETERMINES THE DIRECTION

The natural place of every body for which it is appropriate to leave its natural place and to return to it has a direction determined for and not by this body. This is because such a body may leave its place and come back to it and, in either case, its place has a direction (p. 264).

Therefore it must be that the determination of the direction of this body's natural place is caused by a body other than it, which is only a cause of either that which precedes this body that separates or [that which] is simultaneous with it. Thus that [other] body has a certain priority in the order of existence over this [moving body] by virtue of causality or in another manner.

CHAPTER 4. A FOLLOW-UP: CONCERNING THE CIRCULARITY OF THE BODY THAT DETERMINES THE DIRECTIONS (P. 265)

The body that determines the directions must be either one that surrounds in an absolute manner and has no place, even though it has a position in relation to other bodies (p. 266), [or] one that does not surround in an absolute manner—thus having a place from which it does not separate.

Perhaps the first determinant cannot be other than the first division (p. 267). If the second division had an existence whose place is determined by the first (p. 268), then the place and position of the second would be determined by the first. After that the directions of straight motions are determined (p. 269). It is only appropriate that the first division be prior in the order of creation (p. 270) and have uniform relations of the supposed parts to a certain position. Thus the first division is circular.

CHAPTER 5. REMARK: CONCERNING THE UNDIVERSIFIED NATURE OF THE SIMPLE BODY

A simple body is that whose nature is single and free from (p. 271) the composition of forces and natures (p. 272). A single nature requires that the shapes, places, and whatever else that necessarily accompanies a body be one and the same (p. 273). Thus a simple body does not require [anything] except an undiversified thing.

CHAPTER 6. REMARK: CONCERNING THE CIRCULARITY OF THE SHAPE OF THE SIMPLE BODY

You know that if a body is left to its nature, without the occurrence of a strange, external influence on it (p. 274), it is necessary that it will have a specific place and a specific shape (p. 275). Thus its nature must involve the principle of necessitating this.

A simple [body] has one place that its nature requires, and a composite [body] has [the place that] the dominant [element] in it requires—either absolutely or in accordance with its place (p. 276)—or in whatever [place] it happens to be when the repelling forces in it are in an equilibrium. Therefore every body has one place (p. 277).

A shape required by a simple [body] (p. 278) must be circular; otherwise its forms would be different in one matter, [even though] they are the product of one force.

CHAPTER 7. ADMONITION: CONCERNING THE PROPENSITY OF A BODY FOR MOTION (P. 280)

In its state of motion, the body has a propensity by means of which it moves and which is felt (p. 281) by the resistant.[4] It is not possible for the resistant to resist [a body] except if this propensity in that body is weakened.

This propensity may be due to the nature of the body, or it may occur in the body due to an external influence (p. 282). Thus that which proceeds from the nature of the body[5] is deactivated until [this influence] ceases.[6] Hence [with the ceasing of this influence] the natural propensity returns (p. 283). [An example of this is] the deactivation of the cold, which proceeds from the nature of the body, as a result of the accidental heat to which water is transformed until this heat ceases (p. 284).

The natural propensity necessarily points only in the direction that is desired by the nature [of the body]. Thus, if a natural body is in its natural place, it does not (p. 285) have a propensity while being there. This is because, by its nature, it has the propensity toward its natural place only and not away from it.[7] The stronger the natural propensity, the more resistant is its body to receiving a propensity by violence,[8] and the weaker and slower is the motion by violent propensity.

CHAPTER 8. REMARK: CONCERNING THE NECESSITY OF THE NATURAL PROPENSITY OF A BODY FOR THE VIOLENT MOTION OF THAT BODY

A body that has no propensity, whether in potentiality or in actuality, does not admit of violent propensity by means of which it moves (p. 286). In short, it does not move by violence; otherwise let it move by violence for a certain time over a certain distance and let another body having, for example, a certain propensity and resistance move over the same distance. It is clear that the latter takes a longer time [than the former] to move [by violence] over this distance (p. 287). Also, let the propensity [of a third object] be weaker than the propensity mentioned above, requiring (p. 288) that [third] moving object [to take] the same time[9] [to cross] a distance having the same relation to the first distance that the time of the object with the first propensity has to the time of the object with no propensity (p. 289).[10] Thus [the third object] takes the same time that the object that has no propensity takes to move by violence over the same (p. 290) distance as that of the first. Hence there will be two movements of two objects [that move] by violence—one of which involving resistance and the other not involving resistance—with equal states of rapidity and slowness.

Chapter 9: A Reminder: Concerning the Divisibility of Time

You must remember here that there is no time that is indivisible such that the movement of that which does not have a propensity may occur in it and such that it has no relation to the time of the movement of that which has a propensity.

Chapter 10. Delusion and Admonition: Concerning the Assertion That a Body Has Essentially a Place, a Position, and a Shape (p. 291)

Perhaps you will say that it is not necessary for a body to have essentially a place, a position, or a shape.[11] Rather, one of the bodies may happen to have [a place], a position, or a shape [that become appropriate to it] either at the beginning of its formation—due to that which begins its formation—or due to haphazard external causes that unavoidably affect it (p. 292). For example, every hump of earth happens to have a place appropriate to its nature and is other than that of another hump of earth. This is due to a cause other than its essence, yet aided by its essence.[12] After that, in spite of its various states, it does not separate from a particular natural place that is appropriate to it, [even though] such a place is not required [by its essence] absolutely.[13] The same is true of what is under consideration. The place [of a body] is absolute, even though it is not natural and inseparable from the body in spite of the fact that it is not absolutely required[14] [by the essence].[15] The same can be said of the shape (p. 293).[16]

But, first of all, you must know that everything can be supposed free from foreign qualities that do not constitute its quiddity or existence. Now suppose every body to be such and then reflect whether a position and a shape necessarily accompany it.

As for that which begins the formation, it does not specify for that body at the time of the formation one place rather than another except due to a certain kind of requirement[17] of [its] nature or to a specific motive or haphazardly. If it is due to a requirement[18] [of its nature], then that is that.[19] If it is due to a strange motive other than [that kind of] requirement,[20] then this motive is one of the nonconstitutive qualities. But we have already denied that such qualities are [essential] to a body. Finally, if it is haphazardly, haphazardness is an extrinsic quality. You shall know that haphazardness relies on extrinsic causes.

CHAPTER 11. REMARK: FURTHER CONSIDERATION OF THE BODY'S RELATION TO ITS PLACE AND POSITION (P. 294)

If a body is found in states not necessitated by its nature, its being in such states is among what is possible due to active causes. It naturally accepts change in these states unless met by an obstacle.

If these states pertain to place and position, then it is possible to move away from them in accordance with consideration of the nature. Thus the body would have a propensity.

CHAPTER 12. REMARK: CONCERNING THE CIRCULAR MOTION OF THE ENVELOPING SPHERE (295)

A body that delimits the directions is not such that some of its supposed parts are more fit than some others to have their position and to be along the side [of something else]. Nothing (p. 296) of this is necessary for any such parts, for they are caused [to be where they are by something other than the essence of that delimitant]. Moving away from their [position] is possible, since propensity in the natures of these parts is necessary. This is in accordance with the change in position (to the exclusion of place) that is possible in them—this change being circular.[21] This delimitant, therefore, involves a propensity for circular [motion].[22]

CHAPTER 13. ADMONITION: CONCERNING THE RELATIVITY OF THIS POSSIBLE CHANGE TO AN INTERNAL BODY (P. 297)

You know that this possible change is not in accordance with the relation of some of these parts to some others, but in accordance with their relation either to something external or to something internal (p. 298).

If that body is prior [in existence to any other], then its direction and position are not delimited by an external delimitant that surrounds it. It remains that [this possible change] is in accordance with an internal body.

CHAPTER 14. ADMONITION: CONCERNING THE MANNER IN WHICH THE MOTION OF THE ENVELOPING SPHERE IS MEASURED

You know that during movement[23] the change of a relation may be for the immovable as well as for the movable. [The movement of the enveloping sphere] must, therefore, [be measured in relation to] something immovable.

CHAPTER 15. REMARK: CONCERNING THE PROPENSITY FOR A LINEAR MOTION OF GENERABLE AND CORRUPTIBLE BEINGS

A body that admits generation and corruption is one that has a place before its corruption to (p. 299) another body from which it is generated, and a place after that. This is because every body requires a place appropriate to it.[24] One of the two places is external to the other.

If this body acquires the second form in a place strange to it according to this form, then this requires [the body to have] a propensity for a linear [motion] toward the place that is in accordance with this form (p. 300).[25] If, on the other hand, before it acquires this form, the body is in the place that befits it in accordance with this form, then it must have pushed that which was [in] this place and thus displaced it. Hence the substance of that which was able to take hold of this place is by nature receptive to moving out of its place. Therefore it involves a propensity for a linear [motion]. It follows that every being capable of generation and corruption involves a propensity for a linear [motion].

CHAPTER 16. DELUSION AND ADMONITION: CONCERNING THE ACTUAL LINEAR MOTION OF THE GENERABLE AND CORRUPTIBLE BEINGS

If you are in doubt and say that this being that is generated is adjacent to the body whose form this being took on by generation, then you have affirmed that the kind (p. 301) of the latter falls outside the place of the former, since adjacency is not the place [itself] but [its] neighbor.

CHAPTER 17. REMARK: CONCERNING THE NATURE OF THE ENVELOPING SPHERE AS FREE FROM LINEAR MOTION AND FROM THE TYPE OF GENERATION AND CORRUPTION OF OTHER BODIES

It is impossible for a body involving in its nature a propensity for a circular [motion] to have also in its nature a propensity for a linear [motion]. This is because a single nature does not require steering toward something and turning away from it (p. 302). It has also become clear that that which delimits the directions does not involve the principle of separation from its natural place. Thus it involves no propensity for a linear [motion].

Therefore, this delimitant is among the things whose existence is the product of (p. 303) creation of its maker. It is not among what is generated from a body corrupted to it, nor is it corrupted to a body generated from it. Rather, if it is generated and corrupted, this will be from nonexistence to nonexistence (p. 304). It is for this reason that this delimitant is impenetrable. It does not grow and does not change in a manner affecting its substance, as the heating of water leads to the corruption of water.

Chapter 18. Admonition: Concerning the Primary Bodily Qualities for Acting and Reacting

In the bodies facing us we find powers disposed to act (p. 305) such as heat, cold, stinging, numbing, and many tastes and odors (p. 306). We also find in them powers disposed to react either quickly or slowly. These are exemplified in (p. 307) humidity, dryness, softness, hardness, viscosity, fragility, and compliance (p. 308).

Now, if you search and reflect well, you will find that such bodies may be free of all active powers, with the exception of heat, cold, and that which is in the middle (p. 309) and which in comparison to the hot is cold and in comparison to the cold is hot. I mean by this that you find that in any type of such bodies a body [may] exist devoid of the genus of [certain active powers]. For example, it [may] be without color, odor, or taste. You also[26] find it belonging to heat or cold, such as stinging and numbing.

This is the case with the dispositions prepared for reaction. Research [reveals that] the bodies of this world that surround us are necessarily accompanied by humidity or dryness. This is because easily, and with no resistance, they either separate or conjoin, take on shapes or take off shapes—in which case they are humid, or [they do this] with difficulty—in which case, they are dry. As for those bodies in which this is basically not possible,[27] they are other than these (p. 310).

Regarding [the powers] that resemble these, they are such that a body may be free of them, while belonging to these two [powers] in the manner [that a body belongs to] softness, hardness, viscosity, fragility, and others.

CHAPTER 19. ADMONITION: CONCERNING THE FOUR ELEMENTS

The body that naturally attains the highest degree of heat is fire. That which naturally attains the highest degree of cold is water. That which [naturally] attains the highest degree of fluidity is air (p. 311). And that which [naturally] attains the highest degree of solidity is earth (p. 312). In comparison with water, air is hot and fine. If water is hot and fine, it resembles air (p. 313). If earth is left to its nature and is not made hot by a [certain] cause, it is cold. If fire dies out and its heat separates from it, earthly, solid bodies are formed from it and are pushed around by striking clouds (p. 314).

These four [bodies] have different forms. That is why fire does not settle where air does; nor does water settle where air does; nor (p. 315) does air settle where water does. This is most obvious in the extremities.

CHAPTER 20. ADMONITION: CONCERNING THE CAUSE THAT DETERMINES THE PLACE OF THE ELEMENTS

He who believes that air floats over water—due to the pressure that the weight of water (which collects under it and pushes it upward) exerts on it—and not due to its nature is proven wrong by the fact that (p. 316) the larger [body] has a stronger movement and a faster flotation [than the smaller body]. But that which moves by violence is the contrary of this. The case is the same with the other movements.[28]

CHAPTER 21. ADMONITION: CONCERNING THE COMMON MATTER OF THE FOUR ELEMENTS

A container may cool off by condensation, because of which water drops resembling the dew collect on it. Whenever you wipe them, they extend to any limit you please.[29] These waterdrops are not only in (p. 317) the place where [the container] leaks, nor are they the product of hot water that is finer and more receptive to leaking. Therefore they are air that has been transformed into water (p. 318).

Similarly, it may be clear on peaks of mountains when a cold front hits (p. 319) the air of those peaks, thus condensing it into clouds that do not come to the peaks from somewhere else, nor are they formed (p. 320) from rising vapor. After that these clouds are seen falling as snow that is later stricken by the sunrays, and the process is repeated (p. 321).

Fire may be created by air blows without [another] fire. Also, stony, hard bodies may be transformed into liquid water. Cunning people know this (p. 322). Again, drinking liquid water may be solidified into hard stones.

Thus these four [elements] are capable of transformation from one into the other. Hence they have a common matter.

CHAPTER 22. REMARK AND ADMONITION: CONCERNING THE FOUR ELEMENTS AS PRIMARY PRINCIPLES OF GENERATION AND CORRUPTION IN OUR WORLD

These are the fundamentals of generation and corruption in this world of ours. They are the primary principles. It is appropriate that the number of things having a linear movement is completed by them (p. 323); since there is [1] that which is absolutely light and which is directed upward (p. 324), i.e., fire; [2] that which is absolutely heavy, i.e., earth; [3] that which is light in a nonabsolute manner, i.e., air; and [4] that which is heavy in a nonabsolute manner, i.e., water (p. 325). If you observe all the bodies around us, you will find them belonging, in accordance with the dominance [in them], to one of these [elements] we have enumerated.

CHAPTER 23. ADMONITION: CONCERNING THE MIXTURE OF THE FOUR ELEMENTS AND THE MANNER IN WHICH SUBLUNARY BEINGS ARE GENERATED (P. 326)

Whatever is created is created from these [four elements] due to the temperaments that they involve in (p. 327) different proportions that are disposed toward different constitutions in accordance with the minerals, plants, and animals [as] their genera and species (p. 328). Everyone of these [different constitutions] has a constitutive form from which its sensible qualities arise. A quality may change, while the form is preserved; such as when it happens that water is heated or is subjected to different degrees of solidity and fluidity, while its waterness is preserved (p. 329). While being preserved this form is stable; it is neither strengthened nor weakened. But the qualities that arise from it are contrariwise.

These forms are constitutive of matter, as you have already learned. The qualities, on the other hand, are accidents, and accidents— in whatever manner they are—are accompaniments. That is why forms are not considered accidents (p. 330).

Further, the natural motions and rests of [these forms] are produced by those concealed, natural powers. If [these four elements] are mixed, their powers are not corrupted; otherwise, there will not be [such] mixtures (p. 331). Rather, they will exchange their opposite qualities which are produced by (p. 332) their powers that act upon them, until they acquire a quality having a certain intermediacy, at a certain limit relative[30] to their parts. This intermediate quality is the mixture.

CHAPTER 24. DELUSION AND ADMONITION: CONCERNING CHANGE IN THE QUALITIES (P. 333)

You may say that there is no change in the quality either, as there is no change in the form. Water does not heat up in its substance; rather fiery particles enter it and spread in it. Nor is [the case] as believed, namely, that water cools off. Rather, similarly, ice particles spread in it (p. 334).

If you say so, then consider the case of a rubbed object, a rarified object, and a shaken object when they are warmed up without having a foreign fire reach them. Consider the case of an object heated in an impenetrable [container] and [an object heated] in a penetrable [container] (p. 335). Does the impenetrability prevent the penetration of that which heats by spreading into the object that is heated in proportion with its constitution? Further, does the fullness [of water in a container] closed with its mouth sealed, prevent [the water] from attaining a high degree of heat by averting the spread [of the fiery particles into the water], if nothing [of the water] escapes from the container, thus preparing the way for its replacement by the object that is ready to spread? Consider the case of the explosive sound of long-necked bottles [when placed over strong fire].[31] Again, reflect on how the ice cools what is above it, while its cold parts do not rise due to their heavy weight.

CHAPTER 25. DELUSION AND ADMONITION: CONCERNING THE SOURCE OF COMBUSTION (P. 336)

Or perhaps you will say that the character of fire is latent and is made apparent by the rubbing and shaking without the production of warmth or the character of fire.

Can you believe that the whole—fire that separates from *ghaḍā* wood,[32] which leaves behind the rest of itself spreading in the exterior (p. 337) and in the interior of the firebrands, which is felt spreading into the whole melting glass body, [and which] is clear to vision—is in the wood? If there is nothing of the fire in the wood except that which is left behind in it when it becomes a firebrand, then you will not be able to believe that it is latent in such a manner as not to become apparent [when the wood] is struck or crushed, nor noticeable to touch or to vision. How about [if even the part of the fire that separates were also latent in the wood]? If there is latency and apparency, then most of what is latent becomes apparent and separate. The explication of this is much too long.

CHAPTER 26. A SMALL POINT: REGARDING THE NATURE OF THE FLAME

You must know that the blaze of fire that conceals what is behind it is such only (p. 338) if an earthy thing clings to the fire and acts upon the blaze. That is why the bases of the flame where the fire is found are transparent and without a shade. But that [flame] which is over the bases has a shade due to another lantern [facing it].

The separateness, size, and spreading of that flame may exceed in size that which is transparent. So that one cannot say transparency belongs to spreading, and its opposite to the shape of the pine that produces a compact fire (p. 339). It is clear from this that a simple fire is as transparent as air. If composite fire, of which the stars are formed, is completely transformed into simple fire, it becomes transparent and thus believed to have been extinguished. This is perhaps one of the reasons for its [appearing] around us sometimes as extinguished. It seems that, for the most part, the reason for this around us is the transformation of fire into air and the separation of the earthy compactness into smoke. The stronger the fire, the weaker the smoke becomes. The reason for this is that fire in this state is more capable of completely transforming into itself earthy [elements]. Thus that which is smoke is no longer there as it was in the weak fire (340).

This small point is not appropriate with respect to the species of what is under consideration,[33] but it is appropriate with respect to its genus.[34]

Chapter 27. Admonition: Concerning the Wisdom of the Maker in Creating the Order of Mixtures

Reflect on the wisdom of the Maker. He began by creating principles from which he then created various mixtures. He prepared every mixture for a species and he made the off (p. 341) balance of mixtures an off balance in the perfection of the species. He also made (p. 342) the mixture of a human being closest to the possible balance, so that the human rational soul could dwell in it.

On the Terrestrial and Celestial Souls

CHAPTER 1. ADMONITION: PROOF FOR THE EXISTENCE OF THE SOUL THROUGH INTUITION[1]

Return to yourself and reflect. If you are healthy, or rather (p. 344) in some states of yours other than health such that you discern a thing accurately, do you ignore the existence of yourself and not affirm it? To me this [ignoring and not affirming] does not befit one who has mental vision. One's self does not escape even the one asleep in his sleep and the intoxicated in his intoxication, even though its representation to oneself is not fixed in memory.

Further, if you imagine yourself at the beginning of its creation with a healthy intellect and a healthy disposition,[2] and supposedly it is altogether in such a position and disposition as not to perceive its parts nor have its members in contact—but separate (p. 345) and suspended for a certain moment in free air—you find that it ignores everything except the assertion that it is.

CHAPTER 2. ADMONITION: CONCERNING THE NONINTERMEDIARY MANNER IN WHICH THE SOUL IS APPREHENDED

With what do you apprehend[3] yourself at that time, prior to that time, and posterior to it?[4] Also, what is it of yourself that is apprehended?[5]

Is that which apprehends [yourself] one of your external senses, is it your intellect, or a faculty other than your senses and what belongs to them? If it is your intellect or a faculty other than your senses by which you apprehend [yourself], then do you apprehend [it] by means of an intermediary or without an intermediary?

I do not believe that in that case you are in need (p. 346) of an intermediary.[6] Thus it is without an intermediary [that you apprehend yourself]. It remains, therefore, that you apprehend yourself without the need for another faculty or an intermediary.[7] Hence it remains that you do so by means of your [external] senses or internal [powers] without an intermediary.[8] Reflect further!

Chapter 3. Admonition: Regarding the Nonsensible Nature of the Soul

Do you gather that that which is apprehended of yourself is that [part of] your body that your vision apprehends? No, for if you were stripped of that part of your body, and [if] it were substituted for you, you remain yourself. Or is it what you apprehend by your touch? Again, no, [for] this is nothing other than external members of yourself, whose case is the same as that which was discussed above. Further (p. 347), in the first place, we have supposed that the senses are unaware of their acts.

It is evident, therefore, that that which is apprehended of you is not then one of your organs such as the heart or the brain. How [could it be one of these organs] when the existence of such organs is not revealed to you except through dissection?

Nor is that which is apprehended of you the whole [of your body] inasmuch as it is a whole. This [must be] clear to you from what you observe by yourself and from what you have been warned about.

Therefore, that which is apprehended of you is something other than those things that you may not apprehend when you apprehend yourself and that you do not find necessary for your being yourself.

Thus that which is apprehended of you is not one of the things that you apprehend by the senses in any way, nor one of the things that resemble the senses[9] and that we will mention.[10]

Chapter 4. Delusion and Admonition: The Soul Is Not Asserted by the Mediation of Its Acts (p. 348)

Perhaps you will say: "I assert myself only by the mediation of my act."

You must then have an act that you assert in the previously mentioned assumption or (p. 349) a movement or something else. For, in our consideration of the previously mentioned assumption, we have isolated you from that.

But, with respect to the more general situation,[11] if you assert your act as an absolute one, then from that you must assert an absolute agent and not a specific one—this being yourself in itself. If, on the other hand, you assert your act as an act of yours, you have not thereby asserted yourself by itself. Rather, yourself is a part of the comprehension of your act, inasmuch as it is your act. Therefore yourself is asserted in the comprehension [of your act] before your act. Its being simultaneously [asserted] with it is no less [untrue] than by it. Hence yourself is not asserted by your act.

Chapter 5. Remark: The Soul Is Not the Temperament of the Body, but the Substance That Manages the Body (p. 350)

Here is the human being moving by something other than his corporeality, which [also] (p. 351) belongs to other beings, and by something other than the temperament of his body, which often hinders him in the state of his movement, in the direction of his movement, and indeed, in his movement itself (p. 352). Similarly, his apprehension is by something other than his corporeality or the temperament of his corporeality, which is an obstacle in the way of apprehending what resembles [it] and is changed when encountering an opposite. How then could one apprehend by it?[12]

Because temperament in him occurs among conflicting opposites tending toward disjunction, these opposites cannot be forced into uniting and mixing except by a power other than that which follows upon the union (p. 353) of the temperaments. How [could it be otherwise] when the cause of the union and that which retains the union are prior to the union? So how [could that unifying power] fail to be prior to what is posterior to the union? Whenever weakness or nonexistence follows the uniting and retentive factor, this union undergoes destruction leading to disjunction.

Thus the fundamental powers that move, apprehend, and retain the temperament (p. 354) are something other than [the temperament]. This you may call the soul. This is the substance that (p. 355) manages the parts of your body and hence your body.

Chapter 6. Remark: Regarding the Unity of the Soul and Its Relationship to the Body (p. 356)

This substance in you is one. Rather, when verified, it is found to be you (p. 357). This substance has branches and powers that spread in your organs.

If by some of your organs, you sense something, imagine, desire, or get angry, then the relation between this substance and these branches imposes a disposition on this substance, such that by repetition it produces some submission or (p. 358) habit and character that take hold of the administrative substance as fixed habits do.

Similarly, [this may] happen in a reverse manner. It often begins by the occurrence in [this substance] of a certain mental disposition, then the relation [between this substance and its branches] transports an affection from that disposition to the branches and [from them] to the organs. Reflect on how it is that if you sense the nearness of God, the mighty and illustrious, and think about his omnipotence, your skin shudders and your hair stands at an end.

These reactions and fixed habits may be stronger and they may be weaker. Were it not for such dispositions, the souls of some people would not have been, in accordance with habit, quicker than the souls of some others to become impudent and to flare up with anger.

Chapter 7. Remark: Concerning the Nature of Apprehension (p. 359)

To apprehend a thing is to have its reality represented to him who apprehends such that it is observed by that with which he apprehends (p. 360).

It is either that this reality is the same as the reality of the thing that is external (p. 361) to that which apprehends, when it apprehends—[in which case], it is the reality of that which does not have an actual existence in (p. 362) external, concrete things. This is exemplified in many geometrical figures or (p. 363) by many of the supposed things that are not possible—if supposed in geometry—(p. 364) and that are basically unrealizable (p. 365).

Or the image of the reality of that thing is represented in that which apprehends and is not separate from it (p. 366). This is the remaining [truth].

Chapter 8. Admonition: Concerning the Different Types of Apprehension (p. 367)

A thing may be either: [1] Sensible when observed. [2] After that, it may be imagined when absent, such that its form is represented internally. This is exemplified in Zayd, whom you see and, then, if he is absent, you imagine him (p. 368). Or [3] it may be intelligible, such as when you form from Zayd the concept of human being that is also applicable to others.

When the thing is sensible, it is covered up by veils extrinsic to its quiddity. If these veils are removed from it, their removal will not affect the core of its quiddity. Take, for example, place, position, quality, and quantity in themselves. If one imagines them replaced by other [such qualities], this will not affect the reality of the human quiddity [of Zayd] (p. 369). The senses apprehend the thing inasmuch as it is covered up by such accidents that attach to it due to the matter from which it was created and from which the senses do not strip it. The senses do not apprehend a thing except through a positional relation between their sensation and the matter of that thing. It is for this reason that the form of a thing is not represented in the external senses, if that thing is removed (p. 370).

As for the internal imagination, it imagines the thing accompanied by these accidents and cannot abstract it from them in an absolute manner. But the imagination abstracts the thing from the previously mentioned relation on which the senses rely. Thus the imagination represents the form of a thing even in the absence of that thing's substratum.

Regarding the intellect, it can abstract the quiddity which is covered up by the individuating, strange concomitants, affirming the quiddity as if acting on the sensible in such a way as to render it intelligible (p. 371).

As for that which is in essence free from material attachments and strange concomitants that do not follow upon its quiddity due to its quiddity, it is intelligible in itself and without need of an act by means of which it is prepared as an intelligible (p. 372) for that to which it belongs to have it as an intelligible. Or perhaps it is in proximity from that to which it belongs to have it as an intelligible.

CHAPTER 9. REMARK: CONCERNING THE INTERNAL SENSES (P. 373)

Perhaps you are inclined now to have us give you a minimal explanation concerning the issue of the powers that apprehend internally[13] (p. 374) and to begin first of all with an explanation concerning the issue of the powers that are [most] related to the [external] senses.[14] Listen then.

Do you not see the water drop falling as a straight line (p. 375) and the point that circles with rapidity as a circular line? All this is by way of observation and not by way of imagination or memory. You know that in vision only the form of that which faces [one] is represented (p. 376). That which falls or circles and which faces [one] is something like a point and not a line. There remains, therefore, in some of your powers the form of that which was first represented in vision; the present visual form is [then] conveyed to these powers. Therefore you have a power like the power that observes corresponding to vision and to which vision leads. It is in this power that the sensibles collect and are then apprehended by it (p. 377).

You also have a power that retains the images of the sensibles after the absence [of the sensibles] and as they group in it.

It is by virtue of these two powers that you can judge that this color is other than this (p. 378) taste and that that which has this color has this taste. That which judges these two matters needs to have the two things judged present to it together. Thus these are powers (p. 379).

Animals, be they rational or nonrational, also apprehend particular notions from particular sensibles. These notions are neither sensible nor arrived at by way of the senses. An example of this is the nonsensible notion that the sheep apprehends from the wolf and the nonsensible notion that the ram apprehends from the female sheep. This is a particular apprehension by means of which [this internal power] judges as the senses judge what they observe. Therefore you have a power to which this [function of judging] belongs. Besides, you, as well as many speechless animals, have a power that retains these notions after they have been judged by that which judges them. This power is other than that which retains the forms (p. 380). A specific bodily instrument and a specific name belong to every one of these powers.

The first power is that which is called common sense (al-ḥiss al-mushtarak) or phantasia (banṭāsiā) (p. 381). Its instrument is the spirit that is cast at the basis of the sense nerve, particularly, at the front of the brain.

The second power is called representational power (*al-muṣawwira*) or sensible memory (*al-khayāl*). Its instrument is the spirit that is cast in the interior cavity, particularly in the posterior side.

The third power is the estimation (*al-wahm*). Its instrument is the entirety of the brain; but the [part] most proper to it is the middle cavity (p. 382). In this cavity the estimation is served by a fourth power to which it belongs to compose and divide the forms that follow it and are taken from the senses and the notions that are apprehended by the estimative power. This fourth power also combines the forms with the notions and separates them from each other. If employed by the intellect, this fourth power is called cognition (*mufakkira*) and if employed by the estimative power it is called imagination (*mutakhayyila*). Its power is in the first part of the middle cavity. It is as if it is a certain power of the estimation and, by mediation of the latter, a power of the intellect (p. 383).

The remaining power is memory (*al-dhākira*). Its power is in the location of (p. 384) the spirit that is in the posterior cavity—this cavity being its instrument.

What guides people to the judgment that these are instruments (p. 385) is nothing other than the fact that if corruption affects a cavity in particular [the power cast in that cavity] inherits the defect. Further, the consideration of the necessary in the wisdom of the exalted Maker [requires] the advancing of that which takes hold of the corporeal, putting behind that which takes hold of the spiritual and situating in the middle that which manages (p. 386) both of them by judging and reclaiming the images that evade both sides—great is his power.

Chapter 10. Remark: Concerning the Rational Soul (p. 387)

Likewise the distinction among the powers of the human soul by way of classification is the following: the human soul to which intellection belongs is a substance that has powers and perfections. Among its powers are those that belong to it in accordance with its need for managing the body (p. 388). This is the power for which the name *practical intellect* (al-ʿaql al-ʿamalī) is reserved. This power infers the necessary, particular human affairs that must be done in order to attain by this the chosen purposes from primary premises, well-spread premises, and experiential premises. The theoretical intellect (al-ʿaql al-naẓarī) assists in [giving] the universal opinion from which the soul moves to a particular one.

Among the powers of the human soul, there are also those that belong to it in accordance with its need for perfecting its substance as an actual intellect (ʿaql bil-fiʿl) (p. 389). The first of these powers is one that prepares the soul for [accepting] the intelligibles. A group of people may call this power material intellect (ʿaql hayulānī). This is the niche.

This power is followed by another that occurs to the soul when the primary intelligibles occur to it. With this power the soul is prepared to acquire the second [intelligibles] (p. 390), either by thought, which is the olive tree when it is weak, or by intuition, which is also the oil when it is stronger than that. This power is called habitual intellect (al-ʿaql bil-malaka). It is the glass.

The noble and actual power among these is the saintly one[15] (p. 391) whose oil almost lights up even without being touched by fire.

After that, a power and perfection occur to the soul. Regarding the perfection, it is [acquired by] the soul when the intelligibles occur to it in actuality, in a manner where they are viewed as represented in the mind. This is a light upon a light. As for the power, it belongs to it to obtain the already acquired intelligible, which had been achieved, as that which is viewed whenever the soul desires [to do so] without need for acquisition. This is the lantern.[16]

This perfection is called acquired intellect (ʿaql mustafād) (p. 392), and this power is called actual intellect (ʿaql bil-fiʿl). That which brings out habit into complete actuality and also the material into habit is the agent intellect (al-ʿaql al-faʿʿāl). This is the fire.

CHAPTER 11. ADMONITION: THE DIFFERENCE BETWEEN THOUGHT AND INTUITION

Perhaps you desire now to know the difference between thought (*al-fikra*) and intuition (*al-ḥads*). Listen then (p. 393).

Thought is a certain movement of the soul among concepts. For the most part, it is assisted by the imagination. By means of it the soul seeks the middle term, or what resembles it, of whatever leads to knowledge of the unknown in the case of the absence [of such knowledge]. This is done in the manner of disclosing that which is concealed internally or the like. Sometimes thought leads to the sought object and sometimes it is disrupted.

As for intuition, it presents the middle term in the mind at once, either after search and desire without movement (p. 394) or without desire and movement. Its intermediate, or what is of the same order, is also represented with it.

CHAPTER 12. REMARK: EVIDENCE FOR THE EXISTENCE OF THE SAINTLY POWER

Perhaps you desire to become acquainted with more evidence for the saintly power and the possibility of its existence. Listen then (p. 395).

Do you not know that intuition exists and that people have it in different degrees, as is the case with thought? Some of them are stupid. Thought does not occur to them at all. Some have a certain degree of discernment and enjoy thought. Some others are more cultivated than this and can apprehend the intelligibles by intuition. Such cultivation is not the same in all people. Rather, it can be less and it can be more. As you find the side of deficiency ending to the nonexistence of intuition, be certain that the side neighboring the surplus may end in most of its states to dispensing with learning and thought.

Chapter 13. Remark: Evidence for the Existence of the Agent Intellect and for the Possibility of Our Soul's Conjunction with It (p. 396)

If you desire to have more insight, you must know that it will be made evident to you that [that part] of us [in which] an intelligible form is represented is something other than a body or in a body and that [that in which] the preceding form is represented is a power in a body or a body (p. 397). Further, you know that the sense awareness that a power has of what it apprehends is the representation of that thing's form in it and that, if the form is already realized in the power, that power does not disappear to this form (p. 398). Do you see, if the power disappears to the form and then returns to it and pays attention to it, that something other than the representation of that form occurs in this power? It must be the case then that the form to which the power disappears had been in some way removed from the knowing power. In the estimative power that is in animals, it is possible that this removal occurs in [one of] two ways (p. 399):

The first way is for the form to be removed from this power and from another power—if the latter acts as a store for the former. The second way is for the form to be somewhat removed from this power, yet preserved in another power that acts as a store for the former power. In the first way the form does not return to the estimative power except with the hardship of a new acquisition. But, in the second way, the form may return and become apparent to the estimative power without the hardship of a new acquisition—[if the estimative power] looks over the store and pays attention to it. Something like this is possible in the imagined forms that are preserved in bodily powers. Thus it is permissible that our storage of it is either an organ or in the power of an organ and that inattention to it pertains to another power in another organ. This is due to the fact that our bodies and the powers of our bodies are susceptible to division (p. 400). Perhaps this is not permissible in the noncorporeal. Rather, we say that we find in the intelligibles what resembles these two states. I mean that to which no attention is paid and that which is recaptured.

But the substance in which the intelligibles are represented is, as will be made clear to you, neither corporeal nor divisible. Therefore it does not involve something like a manager and something like a store; nor is it appropriate that it be like a manager and something of the body or its powers be like a store. This is so because the intelligibles are not represented in a body.

It remains, therefore, that there is something external to our substance and contains the intelligible forms in themselves, since it is an actual, intellectual substance (p. 401). If a certain conjunction between our souls and this substance occurs, it imprints on our souls the intelligible forms that are appropriate to that specific preparedness for the appropriate principles. If, on the other hand, the soul turns away from it to what borders the corporeal realm or to another form, that which was first imprinted is then erased. It is as if the mirror by virtue of which one faces the saintly side has been employed to turn away from this intellectual substance to the sensible side or to some other saintly matters.[17] This, too, belongs to the soul only if it acquires the habit of conjunction.

CHAPTER 14. REMARK: THE CAUSE OF CONJUNCTION WITH THE AGENT INTELLECT (P. 402)

The cause of this conjunction is a remote power—this is the material intellect, an acquisitive power—this is the habitual intellect; and a power of complete preparedness to which it belongs to bring the soul, whenever the soul desires, to the direction of illumination by means of a well-established habit—this is called the actual intellect.

CHAPTER 15. REMARK: THE SOUL'S PREPAREDNESS FOR RECEIVING THE INTELLIGIBLES (P. 403)

The soul's multiple managements of the sensible images and the intelligible archetypes, which are in the representational power and in memory [respectively], endow the soul with the preparedness for accepting from the separate substance the abstraction of these images and archetypes due to a certain analogy between them and the soul. This the soul does by employing the power of estimation and that of cognition. Observation of and reflection on this situation verify that this is so (p. 404). Such managements specify the complete preparedness for the forms one by one. An intelligible concept may endow [another] intelligible concept with this specification.

Chapter 16. Remark: Concerning the Immateriality of Intellectual Substances

If you now desire that it be made clear to you that the intelligible notion is not represented in that which is divisible or that which has position, listen then (p. 405).

You already know that an indivisible thing may be joined to a multiplicity of things that do not necessitate this thing to become divisible in position. This is so if the multiplicity of these things is not (p. 406) the multiplicity of that which is divisible in position, such as the parts of the variegated. But a thing that is divisible into a multiplicity having various positions cannot be joined to an indivisible thing. It is inevitable that among the intelligibles there are indivisible concepts, otherwise (p. 407) the intelligibles would be constructed only of principles that are actually infinite, even though it is inevitable that in every multiplicity, be it finite or infinite, there is one in actuality. But if, among the intelligibles, there is that which is one in actuality and is intellected (p. 408) inasmuch as it is one, then it is intellected inasmuch as it is indivisible. Hence [the intelligible] is not represented in that which is divisible in position. [However], every body and every power in a body is divisible.

Chapter 17. Delusion and Admonition: Concerning the Indivisibility of That Which Apprehends the Intelligibles and the Divisibility of That Which Apprehends the Sensibles

Or perhaps you will say that it may be permissible to imagine the intelligible form that is one as divisible into similar parts. Listen then (p. 409).

If each one of the two similar parts is—together with the other—a condition for the completion of apprehending the intelligible form, both parts will be separate from this form as the condition is separate from the conditioned. Further, the intelligible which is intellected only by virtue of two conditions that are its parts will be divided. Again, prior to the occurrence of division, this form will lack the condition and will, therefore, not be intelligible.

If, on the other hand, each similar part is not a condition, the intelligible form in the supposed division will be simultaneously intelligible with that which does not enter in the completion of its intelligibility except accidentally (p. 410). But we have supposed the intelligible form as free from strange concomitants, [yet this asserts that] such concomitants are nevertheless attached to it. How could this be otherwise, when these concomitants occur to it accidentally due to that whose measure of completeness is less than its own?

One of the two parts retains the species of the form—if it is similar. Thus the form (p. 411) we have abstracted is still covered up by a strange disposition for union or separation, increase or decrease, or by specification for a position. Hence this is not the supposed form.

On the other hand, in order for the soul to notice the sensible or representational form, it needs to have (p. 412) the individual parts of this form in different positions and joined to a foreign material disposition (p.413) so that the representation of this form will be in that which has a position and is receptive to division.

CHAPTER 18. DELUSION AND ADMONITION: THE ISSUE OF DIVISION WITH REGARD TO THE INTELLIGIBLES

Or perhaps you will say that the intelligible form will be divided when related to additional ideas, as the one generic idea divides (p. 414) into specific differences and as the one specific idea divides into classified accidental differences. Listen then.

This may be permissible; however, it would involve the attachment of a universal to a universal, which would make the intelligible form another form and not a part of the first form. The essence of the generic intelligible and [that of] the specific intelligible are not divided in their intelligibility [respectively] into specific and classified intelligibles whose totality constitutes the one generic or specific idea (p. 415). Further, the relation of these intelligibles to the divided one idea is not that of parts [to the whole], but that of individual things [to another thing]. If the intelligible idea, which is one and simple and we have already touched upon, divides in some manner into a diversity, this will be other than the manner that was first suspected; i.e., the manner of receiving division into similar elements, in addition to the fact that each of its two parts will be more deserving [than the other] of being the simple element that is the subject of our discourse.

CHAPTER 19. REMARK: TO INTELLECT IS TO BE INTELLIGIBLE

You know that everything that intellects something intellects (p. 416) what it intellects [it] by a power proximate to actuality.[18] This is its intellection of itself. Thus it belongs to anything which intellects something else that it intellects its own self (p. 417). Further, it belongs to the quiddity of anything that is intellected that it be joined to another intelligible. That is why such a thing is also intellected simultaneously with another [intelligible]. No doubt, the rational power intellects this thing only in conjunction [with another intelligible]. If this were one of the things that subsist by themselves, then there is no obstacle from its reality to the conjunction with an intelligible idea (p. 418) except if its essence were afflicted in existence by conjunction with elements—whether material or something else—that obstruct this intellection. If, on the other hand, its reality is free [from such obstacles], its conjunction with an intelligible form is not prevented (p. 419). Thus this [intellection] for it will be possible and (p. 420) will include the possibility of its intellecting itself.

Chapter 20. Delusion and Admonition: Consideration of Intelligibility with Regard to the Material Form (p. 422)

Perhaps you will say that in constitution the material form is free from an obstructing concept when abstracted in the intellect. Why then is intellection not attributed to it?

The answer to your [question] is that it is because it is not independent in its constitution and receptive (p. 423) to the intelligible concepts that reside in it. Rather, what resembles it is joined only to intelligible concepts that are imprinted not [in intelligible concepts] but in that which is receptive to both of them.[19] Neither of them is more deserving of being imprinted in the other than the other (p. 424). Their conjunction is other than the conjunction of the form with that which apprehends the form.

As for its external existence, it is material. But, according to our supposition, the concept under consideration is a substance independent in its constitution. If this substance is joined to an intelligible concept, it has the possibility of applying conception to it.

Chapter 21. Delusion and Admonition: Denial of the Claim That Individuality Is an Impediment to the Intelligibility of the Quiddity (p. 425)

Or perhaps you will say that even if this substance does not have an impediment [for intellection] from its specific quiddity, nevertheless, it has an impediment from its individuality that separates it from its concept, which is imprinted in an intellective power that intellects it (p. 426).

The answer to your [question] is that if the preparedness [for conjunction] of this quiddity were one of the necessary consequences of the quiddity—be the quiddity as it may—then your doubt is removed. But if the substance acquires this preparedness only when representation is made in the intellect, then this preparedness is acquired only with the realization of a representation (p. 427). Therefore, there is no preparedness for a thing until realized, and it then prepares the substance for it, or there is no preparedness for a thing when that thing begins to exist. All of this is impossible. Hence it must be the case that this preparedness is prior to the conjunction. Thus it belongs to the quiddity (p. 428). Indeed, perhaps the specific preparedness of some things that make the conjunction follow the first conjunction.

Similarly, you must know that the quiddity of the generic concept has preparedness for every difference that belongs to it.[20] If this preparedness is not actualized, it is because of an obstacle [that requires] (p. 429) a long discussion. How then [could the preparedness] of the already determined specific concept [be actualized]? This is an answer for another doubt [that may be raised].

Chapter 22. Admonition: Recapitulation

If you study what I have broken down for you into fundamentals, you will know that anything for which it is appropriate to become an intelligible form and which has a subsisting essence is also something for which it is appropriate to intellect. It follows from this that it is appropriate for it to intellect itself (p. 430). Further, anything for which what is appropriate is necessitated by its nature, and for which it is appropriate to intellect itself, is necessary that it intellects itself. This, as well as anything of the sort, does not accept change or substitution.

Supplement to the [Third] Class (p. 431)

On Expositing the Movements Produced by the Soul

CHAPTER 23. ADMONITION: A PREPARATORY NOTE

Perhaps you desire now to hear a discussion about the powers of the soul that produce our actions and movements. Let the following chapters be of this kind.

CHAPTER 24. REMARK: POWERS OF THE PLANT SOUL

The movements of the preservation and generation of the body are managements in the nutritive material intended to assimilate this material in order [1] to replace what has been decomposed; [2] to (p. 432) increase the growth in a purposive proportion that is preserved in the dimensions of the parts of the nourished thing—by means of this, the bodily constitution is completed; and [3] to contract from this nourishment a surplus that is prepared as the matter and principle for another individual. These are three acts of three powers (p. 433). The first is the nutritive power. It is served by [1] that which attracts the nourishment, [2] that which holds what is attracted in order that the attracted be digested by that which digests and breaks into shreds, and [3] that which excretes the residue. The second is the power of growth until completion (p. 434). Growth is other than weight gain. The third is the power of generating the like. It comes into being after the action of the [other] two powers and employs both of them.

However, the power of growth ceases first (p. 435). Subsequently, the power of generation is strengthened for a while and then ceases as well. The nutritive power remains active until it weakens and then the end befalls.

CHAPTER 25. REMARK: MOVEMENTS PRODUCED BY THE ANIMAL SOUL

As for the voluntary movements, they are more animated[21] [than the movements of the plant soul]. They have a principle that decides and determines, and that submits to and is acted upon by the imagination, the estimation or the intellect (p. 436). Either the irascible power that produces harm or the desiderative power that brings about what is necessary or beneficial for the animal proceeds from it. This is obeyed by the moving powers that are cast in the muscles (p. 437) and that serve the power that gives orders.

CHAPTER 26. REMARK: MOVEMENTS OF CELESTIAL BODIES

The movements of the body that has in its nature a propensity for circular [motion] are among the movements of the soul and not those of nature; otherwise, with the same movement, such a body (p. 438) would naturally turn away from what it naturally turns toward, and with its movement it would naturally seek a certain position in the place where it naturally leaves this position and runs away from it. But it is impossible that that which is naturally sought is naturally abandoned, or that that from which one naturally runs away is that which is naturally intended. Rather, this may happen in the volition due to conceiving a certain purpose that requires a diversity of disposition.

Thus it has become clear that the movement of such a body is animated and voluntary.

CHAPTER 27. PREMISE: CONCERNING THE SENSIBLE AND INTELLECTUAL VOLITIONS

The sensible volition is directed toward that which is like the sensible idea (p. 439),[22] and the intellectual volition is directed toward that which is like the intellectual idea.[23] Any idea predicable of many and nonrestricted is intellectual, whether it takes into consideration one individual, as in saying the son of Adam, or does not do so, as in saying human being.

CHAPTER 28. REMARK: CONCERNING THE INTELLECTUAL VOLITION OF THE ENVELOPING SPHERE

By volition, the movement of the first body[24] is not toward movement itself (p. 440). This is because it is not one of the sensible or intellectual perfections. Rather, it is only sought for something other than these perfections. Nothing is more befitting to this movement than position—not a specific and existing position (p. 441), but a supposed one; nor does this movement cease at a specific and supposed position, but at a specific and universal one.

Thus this volition is intellectual. A mystery underlies this.

CHAPTER 29. ADMONITION: CONCERNING THE PARTICULAR VOLITION (P. 442)

A particular individual thing cannot arise from a universal opinion, for such an opinion does not pertain to a particular thing rather than to another, except due to a specifying cause that is inevitably joined to it and not to itself alone.

The animal, which by its animal power seeks nourishment, seeks it and imagines only a particular nourishment, which then produces a particular animal volition (p. 444) and hence by its movement seeks the nourishment that is presented to it only under the aspect of particularity. If, instead of this, another individual [nourishment] were presented to this animal, it would not hate it, but would take it as a substitute.[25]

[However], this does not show that [the particular nourishment] is represented to the animal. Similarly, in crossing a distance, one seeks the particular limits that are represented to one. This representation may be disrupted and it may have some sort of renewed presence, as the movement that retains its continuity is renewed. This does not prevent the individuality and particularity in the representation, as [they are] not prevented in movement (p. 445).

It is in a similar manner that the particular volition is determined; [that is], by a particular thing that brings it into being. The universal volition corresponds to a universal sought object for which it is not necessary to have specification or particularization.

Also, from universal premises, we may draw a universal judgment (p. 446) about what must be done.[26] Then we follow this by a particular judgment that results (p. 447) in a desire and volition that are determined in some form of estimative determination. Subsequently, the moving power proceeds (p. 448) to particular movements that become the object of search due to the first object of search.

CHAPTER 30. RENDEZVOUS AND ADMONITION: MOVEMENT IS DIRECTED TOWARD AN OBJECT WHICH THE MOVER CONSIDERS GOOD FOR IT (P. 449)

The time for the explication of the thing that the first body desires in its voluntary movement will follow the present discourse.

But you must know that if a thing having a voluntary movement moves in search of something it is because it is more appropriate and better for the seeker to have that thing than not to have it—either in reality, in opinion, or in playful imagination; for in that there is a kind of concealed search for pleasure. The absentminded as well as the sleeper act only when imagining a certain pleasure, a change in a certain weary state, or the removal of a certain illness. [While] the sleeper imagines, his organs may also obey the movement resulting from his imagination—no doubt in (p. 450) a state intermediate between sleep and wakefulness or in a necessary thing, such as respiration, or in a thing that comes close to the necessary, as when one sees in sleep a very frightening or a very dear thing that may move one either to flee [from the former] or to seek [the latter].

You must know that the imagination is one thing, awareness of imagination, i.e., that imagination is taking place, is another, and the retention of this awareness in memory is still another thing. It is not necessary to deny the presence of imagination just because one of the other two things is missing.

PART THREE
Metaphysics (p. 5)

On Existence and Its Causes

CHAPTER 1. ADMONITION: DENIAL OF THE VIEW THAT THE EXISTENT IS SENSIBLE

You must know that [some] people's imagination may be overcome [by the opinion] that the existent is sensible, that the existence of that whose substance is not grasped by the senses is supposed impossible, and that that which in itself is not specified by a space or a position, such as the body, or by the cause in which it resides, such as the states of the body, does not have a chance to exist.

It is possible for you to reflect on the sensible itself and learn from this the falsity of the statements of such people; for both you and he who deserves to be addressed know that one name may apply to these sensibles (p. 8) not by way of pure homonymy but in accordance with the same sense, such as the name *human being*. Neither of you doubts that this name applies to Zayd and Amr in the same real sense.

This real sense cannot be such that it is either grasped by the senses or it is not. If it is far from being grasped by the senses, then our investigation has brought what is nonsensible out of sensible things. But this is most astonishing. If, on the other hand, it is sensible, then it necessarily has a position, a place, a specific quantity, and a specific quality. It cannot be perceived or imagined except as such (p. 9); for every sensible object and every imagined object is necessarily specified by something of these states. If this is so, then it will not befit what is not in such a state and thus will not be stated of many things that differ in such a state.

Therefore the human being, inasmuch as his reality is one, rather inasmuch as his primary reality has no diverse multiplicity, is not sensible but purely intelligible. The same is true of every universal.

Chapter 2. Delusion and Admonition: Concerning the Intelligibility of Universal Organs (p. 10)

Perhaps one of them will say that the human being, for example, is such only insofar as he has organs, such as the hand, the eye, the eyebrow, and others. But, insofar as he is such, he is sensible.

We warn him and say that the case of every universal organ[1] that you have mentioned or left out is the same as that of the human being himself.

Chapter 3. Admonition: Further Evidence That the Existent Is Not Sensible (p. 11)

If every existent were such that it enters imagination and the senses, then the senses and imagination would also enter the senses and imagination. The intellect which is the true judge would also enter imagination.

But, after these principles, [we find that] no love, shyness, fear, anger, courage, and cowardice is among that which enters the senses and imagination, [even though] they are among that which attaches to sensible things. What, then, do you think of existent things, if their essences lie outside the order and attachments of the sensibles?

Chapter 4. A Follow-up: The Existence of a Real Being Is Due to the Essential Reality of That Being and Cannot Be Pointed To (p. 12)

Every real [being] is such by virtue of its essential reality, because of which it is real. Thus it is concordant and one [with its essential reality] and cannot be pointed to. What about, then, that by virtue of which every real [being] acquires its existence?

CHAPTER 5. ADMONITION: CONCERNING THE DIFFERENCE BETWEEN THE CAUSES OF QUIDDITY AND THOSE OF EXISTENCE (P. 13)

A thing may be caused in relation to its quiddity or[2] reality, and it may be caused in its existence. You can consider this in the triangle, for example. The reality of the triangle depends on the surface and on the line which is its side. Both the surface and the line constitute the triangle inasmuch as it is a triangle and has a reality of triangularity, as if they are its two causes: the material and the formal (p. 14). But inasmuch as a triangle exists, it may also depend on a cause other than these [two], which is not a cause that constitutes its triangularity and is not a part of its definition. This is the efficient cause or the final cause that is an efficient cause of the causality of the efficient cause.[3]

CHAPTER 6. ADMONITION: REGARDING THE DIFFERENCE BETWEEN ESSENCE AND CONCRETE EXISTENCE (P. 15)

You must know that you understand the concept of triangle while in doubt as to whether or not concrete existence is attributed to triangle. This is after triangle is represented to you as constituted of a line and a surface and is not represented to you as existing.[4]

CHAPTER 7. REMARK: CAUSALITY OF THE EFFICIENT AND FINAL CAUSES

The cause of the existence of a thing, which has causes constitutive of its quiddity, is a cause of some of those causes, such as the form, or of all of them[5] in existence—this is the cause of the union of those causes (p. 16). The final cause, for whose sake a thing is, is in quiddity and idea, a cause of the causality of the efficient cause; whereas in existence it is an effect of it. The efficient cause is a certain cause of (p. 17) the existence of the final cause, if the latter is among the ends that occur in actuality, but it is not a cause of the causality or idea of the final cause.

Chapter 8. Remark: If There Is a First Cause, It Must Be an Efficient Cause for Everything Else That Exists (p. 18)

Thus, if there is a first cause, it is a cause of every existence and of the cause of the reality of every concrete existence.

Chapter 9. Admonition: The Necessary in Itself and the Possible in Itself (p. 19)

Every being, if considered from the point of view of its essence and without consideration of other things, is found to be such that either existence necessarily belongs to it in itself or it does not. If existence belongs to it necessarily, then it is the truth in itself and that whose existence is necessary from itself. This is the Independent Reality. If, on the other hand, existence does not belong to it necessarily, it is not permissible to say that it is impossible in itself after it was supposed existing. But if, in relation to its essence, a condition is linked to it, such as the condition of the nonexistence of its cause, it becomes impossible or, such as the condition of the existence of its cause, it becomes necessary. If no condition is linked to its essence, neither existence nor nonexistence of a cause, then there remains for it in itself the third option, that is, possibility. Thus, with respect to its essence, it would be a thing that is neither necessary nor impossible. Therefore every existent either has necessary existence in essence or has possible existence in essence.

Chapter 10. Remark: The Possible in Itself Cannot Exist Except Due to a Cause Other Than Itself (p. 20)

That to which possibility belongs in essence does not come into existence by its essence, for, inasmuch as it is possible, existence by its essence is not more appropriate than nonexistence. Thus, if its existence or nonexistence becomes more appropriate [than the other], that is because of the presence or absence of a certain thing [respectively]. It follows that the existence of every possible thing is from another.

Chapter 11. Admonition: An Infinite Chain of Possibles Is Possible and Cannot Become Necessary Except Through Another (p. 21)

If that [other] goes on to infinity, every one of the units of the chain will be possible in essence. [But] the whole chain depends on these units. Thus the chain too will not be necessary and becomes necessary through another (p. 22).[6] Let us clarify this further.

Chapter 12. Explication (p. 23)

Every totality having every one of its units as caused requires a cause external to its units. This is because either [1] it does not require a cause at all; hence it is necessary and not possible. But how could this be so when it is only necessitated by its units? [2] It requires a cause that is all its units; hence it is caused (p. 24) by itself.[7] That totality and all [its units] are one thing. Further, *kull* in the sense of "every one" is not something through which the totality is necessitated.[8] [3] It requires a cause that is some of its units. But if every one of its units is caused, then some of its units are not more deserving of being the cause than some others. The reason is that the cause of the caused is more deserving of being the cause. Or [4] it requires a cause external to all its units. This is the remaining [truth].

Chapter 13. Remark: The Cause of a Totality of Units Is First the Cause of Every One of the Units (p. 25)

Every cause of a totality that is something other than its units is, first of all, a cause of the units and then of the totality. If this is not so, then let the units not be in need of this cause. Then, if the totality is completed by its units, it will not need this cause either. Rather, a certain thing may be a cause of some of the units to the exclusion of some [others]. Such a thing is not a cause of the totality in an absolute manner.

Chapter 14. Remark: If a Chain of Consecutive Causes and Effects Includes an Uncaused Cause, That Cause Must Be an Extremity (p. 26)

Every totality organized of causes and effects consecutively, including a noncaused cause, has this uncaused cause as an extremity; for if this cause were an intermediate, it would be caused.

Chapter 15. Remark: Since That Uncaused Cause Must Be a Limit, It Must Be a Necessary Being in Itself (p. 27)

It has become clear that every chain organized of causes and effects, be it finite or infinite, is in need of a cause external to it if it does not include anything save effects. It is necessary that this external cause be linked to it as an extremity.

It has also become clear that if this chain includes an uncaused thing, then this thing is an extremity and a limit. Therefore every chain terminates in that whose existence is necessary in itself.

CHAPTER 16. REMARK: CONCERNING THE RELATION OF THINGS DIFFERING IN CONCRETE EXISTENCE TO THOSE AGREEING IN ESSENCE (P. 28)

All things differing in concrete existence and agreeing in something constitutive of them are such that either [1] That in which they agree is one of the concomitants of that in which they differ. Thus things that differ would have the same concomitant. This is undeniable. [2] That in which they differ is a concomitant of that in which they agree. Thus what necessarily attaches to the one thing would be different and opposite. This is deniable (p. 29). [3] That in which they agree is an accident that occurs to that in which they differ. This is undeniable. Or [4] that in which they differ is an accident that occurs to that in which they agree. This, too, is undeniable.

CHAPTER 17. REMARK: THE EXISTENCE OF A THING CANNOT BE CAUSED BY THAT THING'S QUIDDITY, WHICH IS NOT EXISTENCE (P. 30)

It is permissible that the quiddity of a thing is a cause of one of the attributes of that thing (p. 31) and that one of the attributes of that thing is a cause of another attribute, as the specific difference [is a cause of] property[9] (p. 32). However, it is not permissible that existence, which is an attribute of a thing, be verily (p. 33) caused by that thing's quiddity, which is not existence, or by another attribute (p. 34). This is because the cause is prior in existence, and nothing is prior in existence to existence.

CHAPTER 18. REMARK: PROOF FOR THE UNITY OF THE NECESSARY IN EXISTENCE (P. 36)

That whose existence is necessary is something specific. If its specificity is due to the fact that it is that whose existence is necessary, then there is nothing else whose existence is necessary. If, on the other hand, its specificity is not due to this but to something else, then it is caused (p. 37). This is because [1] if the existence of that whose existence is necessary necessarily attaches to its specificity, then existence necessarily attaches to the quiddity or to an attribute of something other than it. But this is impossible (p. 38). [2] If the existence of that whose existence is necessary is an accident [to its specificity], then it is more appropriate that this existence be due to [an external] cause. [3] If that which specifies that whose existence is necessary is an accident of [its specificity], then that which specifies is also due to a cause (p. 39). If [its specificity] and that by means of which it is specified are one quiddity, then the cause is a cause of the singularity of that whose existence is necessary by essence. But this is impossible (p. 40). [4] Finally, if its occurrence as an accident is posterior to the specificity of a prior first thing, then our discourse is about that prior thing (p. 41) and the remaining divisions are impossible.

CHAPTER 19. A BENEFIT: CONCERNING THE DIFFERENCE AMONG THINGS WITH THE SAME SPECIFIC DEFINITION (P. 42)

One learns from this that things having the same specific definition differ only by causes other [than their specific nature]. If one of these things is not accompanied by the capacity for receiving the influence of such causes—this capacity being the matter—this thing will not be specified except if it belongs to a nature whose species requires the existence of one individual (p. 43). If, on the other hand, it were possible for the nature of its species to be predicable of many, then the specification of every one is due to a cause [other than this nature], for there are no two blacks nor two whites in the same thing, if they do not differ in place and the like.

Chapter 20. A Follow-up: The Necessary in Existence Is Neither a Species Nor a Genus (p. 44)

The conclusion of this is that that whose existence is necessary is one in accordance with the specification of its essence and in no way can it be stated of many.

Chapter 21. Remark: That Whose Essence Is Necessary Is Simple and Indivisible

If the essence of that whose existence is necessary is composed of two or more things that unite, it becomes necessary by them. One of these things or every one of them will be prior to it and a constituent of it (p. 45). Therefore that whose existence is necessary is indivisible, whether in concept or in quantity.[10]

Chapter 22. Remark: A Thing Whose Concept of Essence Does Not Include Existence Derives Its Existence from Something Other Than Its Essence (p. 46)[11]

Everything, the comprehension of whose essence does not include existence, according to our earlier consideration,[12] such that existence is not a constituent of its quiddity. Further, it is not permissible that existence be a concomitant of its essence, as has been made clear.[13] It remains, therefore, that existence is due to something other than its essence.

Chapter 23. Admonition: That Which Is Necessary in Itself Is Neither a Body Nor Dependent on a Body (p. 47)[14]

Everything whose existence is dependent on a sensible body is necessitated by that body and not by its own essence (p. 48). Every sensible body multiplies into matter and form by quantitative division and by conceptual division. Again, for every sensible body, you find another body of its species[15] or of another species,[16] if [considered][17] in relation to its corporeality. [Thus], every sensible body and everything dependent on it is caused.

CHAPTER 24. REMARK: THAT WHICH IS NECESSARY IN ITSELF HAS NO GENUS OR SPECIES (P. 49)

That whose existence is necessary does not share in the quiddity of anything; for any quiddity belonging to anything other than to that whose existence is necessary requires the possibility of existence. As for existence, it is not a quiddity of something nor a part of the quiddity of something. I mean that things having quiddities do not include "existence" in the comprehension of their quiddities. Rather, existence is something that occurs to these quiddities.

Thus that whose existence is necessary does not share a generic or a specific idea with anything (p. 50). Therefore, it does not need to be distinguished from anything by a differential or an accidental idea. Rather, it is distinguished by its essence. Hence its essence has no definition, since this essence has neither a genus nor a difference.[18]

CHAPTER 25. DELUSION AND ADMONITION: REFUTATION OF THE VIEW THAT THAT WHICH IS NECESSARY IN ITSELF FALLS UNDER THE GENUS OF SUBSTANCE (P. 51)

One may think that the idea of the existent that does not inhere in a subject is common to the First and to other things, in the manner that a genus is common; Thus the First falls under the genus of substance.

But this is an error; for the existent that does not inhere in a subject—this being like a description for substance—does not signify that which exists in actuality, such that its existence lies outside a subject; so that he who knows that Zayd in himself is a substance also knows from this that Zayd primarily exists in actuality, let alone the manner of that existence.

Rather, the idea of that which is predicable of substance, such as its description, is something in which specific substances participate (p. 52) when they are in potentiality, as they participate in a genus. It is a quiddity or an essential reality that exists only outside a subject. This predication is applicable to Zayd and to Amr due to their essences and not to [an external] cause. Regarding its being in actual existence, which is a part of its being in actual existence outside a subject, this may belong to it due to [an external] cause. What about, then, that which is composed of it and of an additional idea?

Therefore, that which is predicable of Zayd as a genus cannot be in any way predicable of that whose existence is necessary, because that whose existence is necessary does not have a quiddity that is necessarily accompanied by such a judgment. Rather, necessary existence belongs to it as a quiddity belongs to other things.

You must know that since that which exists in actuality is not stated of the well-known predicables as a genus, it does not become a genus of anything by the addition of a negative idea. Since existence is not one of the constituents of the quiddity, but one of its concomitants, it cannot fall outside a subject [as] a part of a constituent [would], for then it will become a constituent. If this is not so, then, by the addition of an affirmative idea to it, it becomes a genus for the accidents that exist in a subject.

Chapter 26. Remark: That Which Is Necessary in Itself Has No Contrary

The multitude uses *contrary* in the sense of "an opposite equal force." Everything other than (p. 53) the First is caused; but that which is caused is not equal to the necessary Principle. Therefore, there is no contrary to the First in this sense.

The elite, on the other hand, uses *contrary* in the sense of that which shares in a subject consecutively and not simultaneously—if it is naturally at the extreme end.[19] But the essence of the First does not depend on anything, let alone on a subject. Therefore, in no way does the First have a contrary.

CHAPTER 27. ADMONITION: THAT WHICH IS NECESSARY IN ITSELF HAS NO DEFINITION

The First has no alike, no contrary, no genus, and no difference. Thus it has no definition and cannot be indicated except by pure intellectual knowledge.[20]

CHAPTER 28. REMARK: THAT WHICH IS NECESSARY IN ITSELF IS AN INTELLIGENCE THAT KNOWS ITSELF AND IS KNOWN BY ITSELF

The essence of the First is intelligible and independent. Thus the First is self-subsistant, free from attachments, defects, matter, and other things that make the essence in a state additional [to itself]. It has been learned that that of which this statement is true intellects its essence and is intellected by its essence.[21]

CHAPTER 29. ADMONITION: PROOF FOR THE EXISTENCE OF THAT WHICH IS NECESSARY IN ITSELF BY MEANS OF REFLECTION ON EXISTENCE ITSELF (P. 54)

Reflect on how our demonstration of the First's existence, oneness, and detachment from [accidental] qualities does not require reflection on anything other than existence itself, nor does it require consideration of its creation or its acts, even though such things give evidence of it. But [the former] way [of demonstration] is more solid and nobler [than the latter]. That is, if we consider the state of existence, existence attests to the First inasmuch as it is existence. After that, the First attests to all the things that follow it in existence (p. 55).

Something like this is pointed out in the Divine Book: "We will show them our signs in the [various] horizons and in themselves, so that it becomes clear to them that He is the truth."[22] I say that this is the rule for a group of people. The Book continues: "Is it not sufficient that your Lord attests to everything?"[23] I say that this is a rule for truthful people who draw testimony from him [for other things] and not [from other things] for him.

Creation Ex Nihilo and Immediate Creation

CHAPTER 1. DELUSION AND ADMONITION: CONCERNING THE COMMONERS' VIEW THAT ONCE A THING COMES INTO EXISTENCE ITS NEED FOR THE CAUSE OF ITS EXISTENCE CEASES

It appears to the imagination of the commoners that the dependency of a thing,[1] which they call effect, on [another] thing, which they call agent, is in respect of the sense according to which the commoners call the effect an effect and the agent an agent. In this respect the latter brings into existence, fashions, and causes, while the former is brought into existence, is caused, and is fashioned. All this amounts to saying that after nonexistence a thing acquires existence from another thing (p. 58).

They may also say that if a thing is brought into existence, the need for the agent disappears; so that if the agent is missing it is permissible that the effect remains in existence. This is exemplified in their observation of the missing of the builder, while the building still subsists. Many of them do not hesitate to say that if nonexistence were permissible for the Creator, the exalted, his nonexistence would not harm the existence of the world. For the world, according to them, needs the Creator, the exalted, only to bring it into existence, that is, to bring it out of nonexistence into existence. By doing so, he is an agent. But if the world is caused and acquires existence after nonexistence, then, after that, how could it come into existence after nonexistence in a manner in which it would need an agent (p. 59)?

Again, they say that if the world needs the Creator, the exalted, inasmuch as it exists, then every existent needs another thing to bring it into existence. The same would be [true] of the Creator and so on to infinity. We will clarify the manner of this and what must be believed regarding it.

CHAPTER 2. ADMONITION: ANALYSIS OF THE CONCEPT OF ACT

We must analyze the meaning of the expressions *fashions, causes,* and *brings into existence* into the simple elements of their comprehensions, eliminating from them those elements whose inclusion in what is under consideration is accidental (p. 60).

We say that if a thing is nonexistent, and if, then, after nonexistence, it exists owing to a certain thing, we call it an effect. We do not care at this point if any of the two things has the other as its predicate—whether equal [to it] (p. 61), more general [than it], or more specific [than it], so that one would, for example, need to add, saying: "After not existing, it exists owing to that thing—by the movement of that thing with immediacy or through an instrument, by a voluntary design, or not so, i.e., by nature, by generation or by something else, or by what corresponds to these." At present we do not pay attention to these things, since indeed they are additional to a thing's being an effect. That which corresponds to the effect, and due to whose causation the effect exists, is something we call agent (p. 62). What proves this equality [between the agent and the effect] is that if one says, "I acted through an instrument," "through a movement," "through a design," or "by nature," one does not thereby mention something that contradicts the act as an act or that includes a repetition in the comprehension [of the act].

Regarding contradiction, if the comprehension of an act, for example, prevents [the act] from occurring by nature and one says

"I acted by nature," it is as if one says "I acted and I did not act." As for repetition, if the comprehension of an act, for example, includes choice and one says "I acted by choice," it is as if one says "an animal human being" (p. 63).

If this is the meaning of an act, or [if] some [of this] is the meaning of an act, it will not harm us in our purpose, for in the comprehension of an act there are existence and nonexistence. The fact that that existence is after nonexistence is as if this fact is an attribute predicated on this existence (p. 64).

The nonexistence, on the other hand, is not dependent on the agent of the existence of the effect. As the fact that this existence is described as being after nonexistence, that is not due to the action of any agent nor to the making of any maker, for this existence is of something like that for which it is permissible not to exist (p. 65). Therefore, it remains that the dependency [of this existence], inasmuch as it is this existence, is either [the dependency of] the existence of that whose existence is necessary or [the dependency of] the existence of that whose existence must be preceded by nonexistence.

CHAPTER 3. COMPLETION AND REMARK: THE TWO WAYS IN WHICH A THING MAY BE NECESSARY THROUGH ANOTHER

Let us, therefore, consider now on which of these two things [the existence that depends on other things] depends.[2] Thus we say that the comprehension of its being necessary in existence not through itself but through another does not prevent it from being one of two divisions (p. 66). One of them is that whose existence is always necessary through another. The other is that whose existence is sometimes necessary through another. "That whose existence is necessary through another" is predicable of these two divisions, while "that whose existence is necessary through itself" is negated for both of them with respect to [its] comprehension—unless something external prevents this from happening (p. 67).

The existence that is preceded by nonexistence has only one manner [of existing through another]. In comprehension, it is more specific than the comprehension of the former. "Dependency on something else" is predicable of both comprehensions (p. 68). If there are two ideas, of which one is more general than the other, and [if a third] idea is predicated on the comprehensions of both, then that [third] idea belongs primarily to the more general by itself (p. 69) and secondarily to the more specific later on. This is because that idea does not attach to the more specific except if it had already attached to the more general. The reverse is not true (p. 70). So that if it were permissible that the existence of that which is preceded by nonexistence is not necessary through another, and [if it] were possible for it according to its definition, this would not be a dependency.

Therefore it is clear that this dependency is due to the other manner.[3] Because this attribute is a permanent predicate of caused beings, not only in the state of their beginning to exist, it is, therefore, permanent (p. 71). Similarly, if it belongs to its being preceded by nonexistence, then this existence is not only dependent at the time that it is, after not having existed, only so that, afterward, it can dispense with the agent.

Chapter 4. Admonition: Concerning That Which Is Prior to the Generation of Things

That which begins to exist after not having been has a priority in which it does not exist, not like the priority that "one" has over "two," in which that which is before and that which is after can be together in actual existence (p. 72). Rather, it is a priority of a before that does not persist with an after. In a priority of this kind, there is also a renewal of a posteriority after the discontinuity of a before (p. 73).

This priority is not the same as nonexistence, for nonexistence may be after (p. 74); nor is it the agent itself, for the agent may be before, simultaneous with, and after. Therefore this priority is something else in which interruption and renewal persist in a continuity

(p. 75). You had already learned that such a continuity, which corresponds to movements in measures, cannot be composed except of divisible [parts].

CHAPTER 5. REMARK: CONCERNING THE QUIDDITY OF TIME (P. 76)

Because renewal is impossible except with the change of a state, and the change of a state is impossible except for that which has a capacity for the change of a state—I mean the subject—this continuity is then dependent on a movement and a movable—I mean on a change and a changeable thing. But that for which it is possible to continue and not be interrupted is a circular position (p. 77).

This continuity is susceptible to measurement, for a before may be further and a before may be closer. It is, therefore, a quantity that measures change. This is the time (p. 78) that is the quantity of movement, not under the aspect of distance but under the aspect of priority and posteriority that do not coexist.

CHAPTER 6. REMARK: EVERYTHING THAT BEGINS TO EXIST IS POSSIBLE IN EXISTENCE PRIOR TO EXISTING AND IS IN A SUBJECT

Whatever begins to exist must have had possible existence before existing. Thus the possibility of its existence is realized (p. 79). This possibility is not the capacity of that which has power over existing; otherwise, if it were said about the impossible that one has no power over it because it is not possible in itself, it would have been said that (p. 80) one has no power over it because one has no power over it or that it is not possible in (p. 81) itself because it is not possible in itself. It is clear, therefore, that this possibility is other than (p. 82) the fact that that which has power over existing has power over existing (p. 83).

Nothing intelligible in itself has its existence outside a subject. Rather, it is relative and thus in need of a subject (p. 84). Hence that which begins to exist is preceded by a power to exist and by a subject.

Chapter 7. Admonition: Essential Posteriority of Possible Things

A thing may be posterior to another in many ways, such as the posteriority of time and that of space. Now we do not need [to consider] in the group [of posterior things] anything except that which is required by existence, even though it is not impossible that it be in time simultaneous [with that which is prior to it in existence]. This happens when the existence of a thing is from (p. 85) another and the existence of that other is not from it. The former does not merit existence except after the latter has already realized actual existence (p. 86). The former does not mediate in existence between the latter and another thing; rather, existence comes to the latter, not from the former. Existence does not reach the former except after having already reached the latter (p. 87). This is exemplified by your saying: "I moved my hand, thus the key moved" or "following that, the key moved." You do not say: "The key moved, thus my hand moved" or (p. 88) "following that, my hand moved." This is in spite of the fact that both things [moved] simultaneously in time. This posteriority is with respect to the essence.

You also know that the state of a thing that belongs to the thing according to that thing's essence, and not according to anything else, is essentially prior to the state of the thing that is derived from something other than the thing itself (p. 89). Whatever exists owing to something other than itself merits nonexistence if isolated, or existence does not belong to it if isolated. Rather, existence belongs to it only due to something else (p. 90). Therefore it has no existence before it has existence. This is the essential beginning of existence.

Chapter 8. Admonition: Once a Thing Is Complete as an Actual Cause, Its Effect Is Made Necessary

The existence of the effect depends on the cause, inasmuch as the cause is in a state by virtue of which it is a cause, such as the state of nature, volition, or some further thing that must be one of the external things that take part in the completion of the cause as an actual cause. Such things are exemplified by [1] the instrument, [as in] the carpenter's need for the hammer (p. 91); [2] the matter, [as in] the carpenter's need for wood; [3] the assistant, [as in] the sawyer's need for another sawyer; [4] the time, [as in] a human being's need for the summer (p. 92); or [6] the removal of an obstacle, [as in] the washer's need for the removal of heavy rain (p. 93).

The nonexistence of the effect depends on the nonexistence of the cause in a state by virtue of which it is an actual cause, whether the cause itself exists, but not in that state, or whether it does not exist at all. If there is no external impediment, and [if] the agent itself exists, yet without being a cause by essence, the existence of the effect will depend on the existence of the aforementioned state. Thus, if such a state exists, whether as a nature, as a decisive volition, or as something else, the existence of the effect is made necessary. If, on the other hand, such a state does not exist, the nonexistence of the effect is made necessary. If the existence or the nonexistence of such a state is assumed to be forever, that which corresponds to it will also be forever. [If it is assumed to be for] some time, that which corresponds to it will also be for some time. If it is permissible that a thing has a uniform state eternally,[4] and it has an effect, it is not far-fetched that this effect will necessarily follow from it eternally (p. 94).[5] Therefore, if this is not called an effect because it is not preceded by nonexistence, there is no problem of naming since its meaning has become clear.

Chapter 9. Admonition: On the Meaning of Al-Ibdā' (p. 95)

Immediate creation (*al-ibdā'*) is a thing's giving existence to another that depends on nothing other than it—without the mediation of matter, instrument, or time. That which is preceded by temporal nonexistence, on the other hand, cannot dispense with an intermediary. Immediate creation is in a nobler rank than material production (*al-takwīn*) and temporal production (*al-iḥdāth*).

Chapter 10. Admonition and Remark: The Existence of Things Possible in Themselves Is Necessitated by Their Cause (p. 96)

It is evident to the first intellect that the tipping of balance of one of the two extremities of the possibility of anything[6] that had not existed and then existed became preferred [over the other extremity] owing to a certain thing or a cause, even though it may be possible for the [human] mind not to pay attention to this evidence and to resort to [other] kinds of proof (p. 97). This tipping of balance and appropriation owing to that thing occurs either after being already necessitated by the cause or without yet being necessitated, but made by the cause in the realm of possibility, since in no way is this tipping of balance prevented from being produced by the cause. Thus we return to the original state of seeking the cause of the tipping of balance once again, and to this there will be no succession. Therefore the truth is that the tipping of balance is necessitated by the cause.[7]

Chapter 11. Admonition: Owing to Its Indivisible Reality, the One Can Produce Only One Thing

The comprehension of a certain cause inasmuch as (a) necessarily follows from it is other than the comprehension of a certain cause inasmuch as (b) necessarily follows from it (p. 98). If that which is one necessarily produces two things, this is in virtue of two aspects different in comprehension and in reality (p. 99). These two aspects are either among the constituents of that which is one, its necessary concomitants, or [its] individuating elements (p. 100). If these two aspects are assumed to be among the necessary concomitants of that which is one, once again the search goes back to the original case. Thus you are led to two different aspects among the constituents of the cause (p. 101), owing either to [its] quiddity or to its existence (p. 102) or to [its] individuating elements.[8] Therefore every being that necessarily produces two things simultaneously, of which neither is mediated by the other, has a divisible reality.[9]

CHAPTER 12. DELUSIONS AND ADMONITIONS: CONCERNING THE DIFFERENT VIEWS REGARDING THE NECESSITY AND POSSIBILITY OF THINGS

A group of people said that this sensible thing exists by its essence and is necessary by itself (p. 103).[10]

But, if you recall what was mentioned to you concerning the condition for that which is necessary in existence, you will not find this sensible thing necessary and will recite the saying of God, the exalted: "I do not love those things that disappear."[11] For that which is at the bottom of the realm of possibility is a certain [kind of] disappearing.

Others said: "Rather, this sensible existent is caused." Then they differed (p. 104). Some of them claimed that its principal element and matter are not caused, but its makeup (ṣunʿatah) is caused. Thus this group posits two necessary beings in existence. You are well aware, however, of the impossibility of that.

Others of them attributed the necessity of existence to two contraries or to a number of things and considered everything else as derived from that (p. 105). This group is of the same judgment as those before them.

Others agreed that that whose existence is necessary is one; then they differed [among themselves]. A group of them said that it continues without the existence of anything resulting from it. Then it began to desire the existence of something from it (p. 106). Were it not for this, the renewed states of various types would have had an infinite past, [but] they exist in actuality. This is because every one of them exists; therefore all of them exist. Thus a totality limited in existence belongs to an infinity of succeeding things.

They say but this is impossible. If there is a totality that limits its parts together, it falls under the same judgment. How could one of these states be described as (p. 107) not existing except after that which is infinite, such that it becomes dependent on [the passage of] that which is infinite, and thus that which is infinite becomes interrupted at it? Following that, every time this state is renewed the number of those states is increased. But how could the number of that which is infinite be increased?

Of this group there are those who said that the world existed since it is better by existing [than by not existing] (p. 108). Others said that the existence of the world is impossible except at the time it existed. Still others said that the existence of the world does not depend on a time or on any other thing, except on the agent. However, they do not inquire about [the reason for] acting or not acting. Thus this group is the same as that group. Contrary to these, there is a group that asserts the unity of the First. They say all the primary attributes and states of that whose existence is necessary through itself also have necessary existence (p. 109) and that, in pure nonexistence, no state can be distinguished in which it is more appropriate for the First not to bring into existence anything or for things not to be primarily produced by the First or an opposite state.

Furthermore, it is not permissible that a renewed volition arises except due to a motive, nor that it arises carelessly. Similarly, it is not permissible that a nature or something else arises without the renewal of a state [of the agent] (p. 110). How would a volition arise due to a renewed state when the state of that which is renewed is the same as that which prepares the renewal for it—the latter being renewed? If there is no renewal, the state of that for which there is no renewal will be one and the same state that continues in the same manner—whether you consider the renewal as belonging to something present or to something (p. 111) that has already been removed. This is exemplified by the beauty of the action whenever present, or at a determined time, or in some other manner that has already been enumerated, or by the ugliness that had belonged to the action or had been removed, or an obstacle, or something else that was but was removed (p. 112).

They say that if the motive that hinders that whose existence is necessary from flowing into goodness and excellence is that the effect is necessarily preceded by nonexistence, then this motive is weak. Its weakness has already been revealed to the just minded, since it subsists in every state and is not more deserving of the affirmation of priority in one state than in another (p. 113).

Regarding the effect as having possible existence in itself and necessary existence through another, this does not contradict its having permanent existence through another, as you have already been told.

As for that which is infinite being an existing totality due to the fact that every one [of it] has existence at a certain time, this is a false opinion. This is because if a judgment is true of every one it is not [necessarily] true of the realized totality; otherwise it would be proper to say that it is possible for an infinite totality to enter into existence because it is possible for every one [of it] to enter into existence. Thus possibility would be predicated of the totality as it is predicated of every one [of the totality].

They say that infinite states they have mentioned do not cease to be nonexistent, [not to come into existence] except one thing after another (p. 114), and the nonexistent infinite may involve more or less without this causing a breach in the states that are infinite in nonexistence.

Regarding the dependency of one of these states on having prior to it that which is infinite, or the need of some of these states for having that which is infinite interrupted at reaching it, this is a false view. This is so because the meaning of our statement, "Such and such depends on such and such," is that the two things together are described as nonexistent and the existence of the second cannot be except after the existence of the first nonexistent.

The same is true of need. Furthermore, it is never true to say at any one time that the latter depends on the existence of that which is infinite or has need for (p. 115) that which is infinite to reach it. Rather, [if] you suppose any time, you will find between it and a later one, finite things.

Thus, at all times, such is its attribute, especially as the totality is present to you and every part [of it] is one.

If by this dependency you mean that this [thing] does not exist except after the existence of things—every one of which being at a different time—then it is not possible to count the number of such things. This is absurd, for this is the same thing under dispute, namely, whether or not it is possible. How then could it be a premise in the refutation of it? Is it by changing the expression in a way that does not change the meaning?

Therefore the consideration of what we have pointed out requires that the Artisan (p. 116), the Necessary in existence, does not have different relations to the [diverse] times and things that derive their existence primarily from it and to the essential consequence of this consideration, except as necessarily resulting from a diversity followed by change.

These are the doctrines. Choose [among them] in accordance with your intellect, and not your passion, after having posited that the Necessary in existence is one.

On Ends, on Their Principles, and on the Arrangement [of Existence]

CHAPTER 1. ADMONITION: THE MEANING OF "COMPLETE RICHNESS" (P. 118)[1]

Do you know what enjoys complete richness? It is that which is not dependent on anything external to it in three things: in its essence (p. 119), in dispositions that take hold of its essence, and in perfective dispositions in relation to its essence. Thus that which is in need of something external to it in order to have a complete essence (p. 120), or of a state that takes hold of its essence, such as figure, beauty or something else, or of a state that has a certain relation, such as knowledge or the capacity for knowledge and power or the capacity for power (p. 121), is poor and in need of acquisition.

CHAPTER 2. ADMONITION: GOD'S PERFECTION DOES NOT DEPEND ON HIS CREATION (P. 122)

You must know that a thing for which it is best only if another thing is produced by it, and whose production is more befitting and more appropriate than its nonproduction, is such that if that other thing is not produced by it then that which is absolutely more befitting and better for it is not. Also that which is relatively more befitting and better for it is not. Therefore it is denied a certain perfection—this renders it in need of acquisition.

Chapter 3. Admonition: God and Other Exalted Beings Cannot Seek to Do Something Good for What Is Below Them (p. 123)

How abominable it is to say then that exalted things try to do something for what is below them since that is better for them and, in order to be agents of good deeds since that is among what is good and appropriate for noble things, that the First, the True, does something for the purpose of another and that there is a reason for its action.[2]

Chapter 4. A Follow-up: The Meaning of "Real King" (p. 124)[3]

Do you know what a king is? The real king is the absolutely real rich one, the one with which nothing can dispense in any matter, and the one to which the essence of everything belongs. This is because everything is from it or is among those things whose essence is from it. Thus everything other than it is in its possession and it has no need for anything.

Chapter 5. Admonition: The Meaning of Generosity (p. 125)

Do you know what generosity is? Generosity is providing a benefit that must be[4] for no compensation.[5] Therefore perhaps one who gives a knife to him who must not have it is not generous. Also, one who gives in order to obtain compensation from him with whom one is dealing is not generous (p. 126). Not all compensation is [for] the same thing, but [it may also be for] something else, [such as] even gratitude, praise, getting rid of blame and attainment of the better and what must be.

Thus one who gives generously in order to be honored or thanked,[6] or in order to acquire some good from one's act, is the one who seeks compensation and is not generous (p. 127). Hence the real generous one is the one from whom benefits flow, not due to a desire in him nor to an intended search for something that will come back to him. You must know that one who does something, [because] if one does not do it, it will be bad for him or it will not be good for him, then one [seeks] to derive a compensation from one's act.

Chapter 6. Remark: Exalted Beings Do Not Have an End in What Is Inferior to Them, and God Has No End in Anything (p. 128)[7]

The exalted does not seek something for the sake of that which is base, so that the base would be an end for the exalted. That which is an end may be distinguished from its opposite with respect to choice (p. 129). According to the choice maker, that which is an end is more befitting and more needed [than not], so that if it were true to say of it that, in itself, it is more befitting and better [than not], but it is not such that according to the agent seeking it and desiring it that it is more befitting and better for the agent [than not]; then it is not an end. Therefore, the generous and the real king has no end, and the exalted does not have the base as an end.

Chapter 7. Admonition: A Being That Has No Movement and No Volition Seeks No End in Anything Else[8]

Anything that has a permanent movement by volition anticipates one of the above-mentioned ends that gives back to it [things], including its being good or deserving of praise. Hence the action of that which is above this is above movement and volition.

Chapter 8. Delusion and Admonition: The Rich Is Necssitated to Do the Good by the Intrinsic Nature of the Good (p. 130)[9]

You must know that what is said concerning good action, namely, that its being necessary and good in itself is something that does not enter in its being chosen by the rich[10] except if doing that good raises the rich above imperfection, glorifies him, and purifies him; while abandoning it creates in him deficiency and rapture. But all of this is contrary to the rich.

CHAPTER 9. REMARK: CONCERNING THE FLOW OF THE UNIVERSAL ORDER OF EXISTENCE FROM DIVINE KNOWLEDGE (P. 131)

If you make a sincere search, you will find nothing to say except that the representation of the universal order in the [divine] preknowledge together with its necessary and appropriate time is the thing from which that order, with its organization and details, flows in an intelligible manner (p. 132). All this is providence (p. 133) This is a summary, to the details of which you will be guided later.[11]

CHAPTER 10. ADMONITION: CONCERNING THE EXISTENCE OF THE SEPARATE CELESTIAL INTELLIGENCES (P. 134)

It had become clear to you that the celestial movements depend on a universal volition and on a particular volition.[12] Further, you know that the principle of the universal and absolute first volition must be a separate intellectual essence (p. 135). If this volition perfects [its] substance by its own virtue, it will not be accompanied by insufficiency. Thus it will be a volition resembling the already-mentioned providence.

You know that that which is universally intended is not one of the things that are renewed and severed, whether in an interrupted or a continuous manner. Rather, it has either (p. 136) a realized nature or a nonexistent nature.[13] It is not permissible to say concerning permanent things that something that belongs to them has not ceased to be absent and then was realized. Again, it is not permissible to say that such a thing has not ceased to be realized, yet it is sought. On the contrary, all the perfections of permanent things are present and real.

They are neither particular nor conjectural nor imaginary. Further, the relations of that which resembles the things we have mentioned to the celestial bodies are not the same as the relations of our souls to our bodies in producing one animal, as is the case with us. This is because the soul of any one of us is linked to his body insofar as (p. 137) the body is complete, in order to seek from it the principles of perfection. Were it not for this, our soul and body would have been two separate substances.

As for the soul of the heavens, it possesses either a particular volition or a universal volition on which it depends for acquiring a kind of perfection—if the soul of the heavens [possesses a universal volition]. In this there is a mystery.

CHAPTER 11. REMARK AND ADMONITION:
CONCERNING THE FINAL CAUSE
OF THE CELESTIAL MOVEMENT (P. 138)[14]

Nor is it possible to say that the soul of the heavens' movement of the heavens is due to a desiderative or to an irascible motive. Rather, this movement must resemble our movements, which are produced by our practical intellects (p. 139). It is unavoidable that this soul's movement is directed toward a loved and chosen object in order to attain either the essence of this object, [one] of its states, or something that resembles these two things (p. 140).

If the movement is directed toward the first, it ceases when attaining [its object]; otherwise it seeks the impossible (p. 141). If the movement is for the purpose of seeking to attain resemblance, inasmuch as that is stable, then, due to seeking attainment of the resemblance, it is unstable. Thus it does not attain its perfection except in a [continuous] succession resembling perpetual interruption—this is if [the individuals] that undergo a numerical change retain their species by succession. Every number (p. 142) that is supposed to belong to what is in potentiality is then undoubtedly actualized and its species or type is preserved by succession.

Thus that which desires has resemblance to things in actuality—inasmuch as such things are free from potentiality—such that the good flows from it, as the good flows inasmuch as the resemblance is to the exalted and not inasmuch as it is a flow over the lower object. The principle of this lies in the [different] states of position that dispose the flow. Whatever is in potentiality in the heavens follows the same course, just as that of the actual inasmuch as this is possible by succession.

CHAPTER 12. ADMONITION: CONCERNING THE MULTIPLICITY OF THE SEPARATE INTELLIGENCES (P. 143)[15]

If the resembled object were one, then resemblance in all the celestial [bodies] would be one, but it is different (p. 144). If it belonged to one of these [bodies] to resemble another, it would resemble it in method, but this is not the case except rarely.

CHAPTER 13. DELUSION AND ADMONITION: THE MANNER IN WHICH THE FIRST CAUSE AND THE CELESTIAL INTELLIGENCES ARE IMITATED (P. 145)

A group of people believe that the resembled object is one only and that it would have been permissible for the movements to resemble one another. But since it was the same for them to move in any haphazard direction, as a result of which the end is reached by the movement (p. 146)—further, [since] it was possible for them to seek movement in a manner beneficial to the objects under them, even though the movement is not primarily for that purpose—they combined the movement due to that which motivates them to move toward the end with the direction of this movement in a beneficial manner (p. 147).

We say that if it were permissible to expect the manner of the movement to benefit the inferior objects it would also be permissible to expect this from the movement.

Someone may say that since it belongs to the celestial bodies to be in motion and to be at rest—the two things being equal for them, as are the two directions of the two movements—further, if their being in motion is more beneficial to the inferior objects [than their being at rest], they choose being in motion (p. 148). Rather, if the celestial bodies do not primarily act for the sake of the inferior objects, but seek only higher objects—something that results in benefit—then the manner of the movement must be the same. If this is so, a variation occurs there due to a cause prior to that which is beneficial and follows upon the variation. Therefore what is resembled are things different in number, even though it was permissible that the first resembled object be one for whose sake movements are similar in that they are circular.

Chapter 14. Additional Insight: Whether It Is Possible for Human Beings to Grasp This Resemblance (p. 149)

It is not for you now to demand of yourself the grasping of the nature of this resemblance after you have understood it in general; for when the human faculties are in the world of exile they fall short of grasping the nature of what is below this resemblance. So how [could they grasp the nature of] this resemblance?

Allow that, if the mover desires a resemblance by means of which it renewably acquires something, a reaction of seeking permanence that is appropriate to the resemblance occurs in the mover's body, similar to the reactions that occur in your body as a result of reactions in your soul (p. 150).

If you seek the truth by making an effort concerning it, a mystery may be revealed to you clearly [after it has been] concealed. Thus make an effort and learn how this is possible, and that these reactions are dispositions resembling images and not purely intellectual—even though they are images produced by what is purely intellectual with respect to the preparedness of those bodily powers (p. 151). When the intelligibles are revealed in yourself, you realize by your imagination a resemblance to them with respect to your preparedness, and perhaps they lead to movements of your body.

If you desire another kind of evidence pertaining to what is under consideration, listen then.

CHAPTER 15. ADMONITION: CONCERNING FORCE AS AN ESSENTIAL ACCIDENT OF THE FINITE AND THE INFINITE

Force may be exerted on finite actions, such as the moving of the force that is in a hump of earth (p. 152). It may also be exerted on infinite actions, such as the moving of the force that belongs to the heavens. The former is called finite (p. 153), and the latter infinite, even though *finite* and *infinite* can be said in senses other than these two.

CHAPTER 16. REMARK: THE MOVEMENT THAT PRESERVES TIME IS CIRCULAR

The movements that impose limits and points are those by virtue of which arrival [to] and attainment [of an end] occur due to a mover that produces the arrival and that actually produces the arrival at the time of the arrival (p. 154). The arrival is not the same as separation, movement, or any other thing that does not occur at a [specific] time (p. 155). The mover ceases to be something that produces the arrival any moment the movable is separate from the limit (p. 156). It becomes something that does not produce the arrival at once, even though it rests for a while, not as a thing is (p. 157) separate and moves (p. 158). The time at which the mover becomes something that does not produce arrival at once is other than the time at which it becomes something that produces arrival at once (p. 159). Between these two times there is a time at which the mover is something that produces arrival—this is no doubt rest (p. 162).

Thus every movement over a distance leading to a certain limit leads to rest in that limit (p. 163). Hence it is different from the movement by means of which continuous time is preserved. Therefore positional movement is that by means of which continuous time is preserved—this is circular movement.

CHAPTER 17. BENEFIT: BEING A MOVER IS SIMULTANEOUS WITH BEING NONPRODUCTIVE OF ARRIVAL (P. 164)

It must only be said that the mover has become nonproductive of the arrival, and it must not be said, as they say, that it has become separate. This is because movement and separation, which is the movement that is attributed to that which moves away from the end, do not occur at once, nor do they involve either that which is a first movement or separation. But the mover's ceasing to be productive of the arrival occurs at once.

CHAPTER 18. A FOLLOW-UP: A MOVEMENT WITH AN INFINITE FORCE IS CIRCULAR (P. 165)

Thus the movement in which one seeks the mode of force, inasmuch as it is infinite, is the circular movement.

CHAPTER 19. REMARK: A CORPOREAL FORCE CANNOT BE INFINITE AND CANNOT HAVE AN INFINITE DRIVING MOTION BY VIOLENCE

You must know that it is not permissible for a body with an infinite force to move another body. This is because the latter cannot be but finite (p. 166). If, by its force, the former produces in a certain body movements that are infinite in power due to a principle we suppose (p. 167), and then we suppose that by the same force it moves a smaller body due to the supposed principle, it must then move the smaller body more than it moves the larger one (p. 158). Thus the surplus in force falls in the other side,[16] whereas[17] the other side[18] also becomes finite[19] (p. 169). But this is impossible.[20]

Chapter 20. A Premise: A Corporeal Force Cannot Have an Infinite Driving Motion by Nature Either (p. 170)

If a certain body moves a body in which there is no resistance, the larger and the smaller bodies will have equal receptivity to movement. Neither of them will be more resistant or more ready [to being moved than the other], since there is no obstacle at all [in either of them].

Chapter 21. Another Premise: A Body's Receptivity to Movement Is Due to That Body's Force, Not to Its Size (p. 171)

If the natural force of a certain body moves its body when its body does not involve any obstacle, it is not permissible that a difference in receptivity [to movement] occurs due to [the size of] the body. Rather, this is apt to occur due to the force.

Chapter 22. Another Premise: Concerning Similarity of Corporeal Forces in Bodies Different in Size

If the force in a larger body resembles that in a smaller body—so that, if one takes [a portion of] the larger body equal [in size] to the smaller body (p. 172), the two forces will be absolutely similar, then the force in the larger body will be stronger and more abundant [than that in the smaller body] since the former has a force similar to that [of the latter] plus an addition.

Chapter 23. Remark: A Body Cannot Have a Natural Force That Moves That Body to Infinity

We say that it is not permissible to have in any body a natural force that moves that body without finitude. This is because the force of that body is more abundant and stronger than the force of the parts of that body when they are isolated (p. 173). The addition in force that the body of these parts involves does not affect the resistance to moving, so that the relation of the two movables [to] the two movers becomes one. Rather, the two movables are in the class of things that do not differ while the two movers differ. If the two movers move their bodies in an infinite manner by a supposed principle, then what we have already mentioned occurs (p. 174).[21] If the smaller body is moved by finite movements, the addition [that the larger body has] over the movements of the smaller one will be in a finite relation. Thus all will be finite.

Chapter 24. A Follow-up: The Infinite Force Moving the Heavens Is Separate and Intellectual (p. 175)

It follows from this that the force moving the heavens is infinite and noncorporeal Therefore it is separate and intellectual.

Chapter 25. Delusion and Admonition: The Difference Between the Proximate and the Remote Movers of the Heavens (p. 176)

Perhaps you will say: You have held that the heavens move due to a separate [mover], while before that you had not allowed that the direct [principle of] movement is a pure intellectual thing, but [said] that it is a corporeal force.[22]

The answer to you is that what has been confirmed [in the last chapter] is a primary mover, but it is permissible that the adherent mover be a corporeal force.[23]

CHAPTER 26. DELUSION AND ADMONITION: REFUTATION OF THE VIEW THAT IF THE PROXIMATE MOVER OF THE HEAVENS IS A CORPOREAL FORCE IT WOULD HAVE A FINITE AND NOT A PERPETUAL MOVEMENT AS IS THAT OF THE HEAVENS (P. 177)

Perhaps you will say: If this were permissible, the direct mover of the heavens would have a finite and not a perpetual movement. Thus it would be [a mover] of a movement other than that of the heavens. Listen then.

You must know that a mover having an infinite movement moves something else and then that other thing produces infinite movements, not inasmuch as movements are produced by it when it is isolated, but inasmuch as it has not ceased to be affected and to act by that first principle (p. 178).

You must know that receiving infinite actions is other than [receiving] infinite influences, and infinite influences by way of mediation are other than infinite influences by way of a principle. In bodies only one of these three is prevented.[24]

CHAPTER 27. REMARK: CONCERNING THE ORIGIN AND MANNER OF THE FLOW OF THE STATES OF THE CELESTIAL SOULS AND THE CELESTIAL MOVEMENTS THAT RESULT FROM THESE STATES (P. 179)

Thus the intellectual, separate principle is such that physical movements that belong to the celestial soul do not cease to flow from it in a desiring, psychical manner from which the celestial movements are produced in the manner of production already mentioned. Because the influence of the separate [principle] is continuous, whatever is a consequence of this influence is also continuous. Indeed,[25] the first mover is separate [in the most primary sense]. Nothing but this is possible.

CHAPTER 28. DRAWING TESTIMONY: ARISTOTLE'S ASSERTION REGARDING THE NONCORPOREAL INFINITE FORCE OF THE MOVER OF EVERY SPHERE AS THE SOURCE OF AN INFINITE MOVEMENT OF THAT SPHERE

The father of Peripatetics had attested that the mover of every sphere emits [to that sphere] an infinite movement (p. 180) and that its force is infinite; [therefore] it is not in a corporeal force. But many of his followers did not pay attention to him and believed that the movers that come after the first may move accidentally because they are in bodies. It is astonishing that they have attributed to these movers intellectual conception without being aware that intellectual conception is not possible for a body (p. 181) or for the force of a body. Thus it is not possible for that which moves by its essence or for that which moves accidentally, i.e., by a cause movable by its essence. If you determine the truth, you will not permit yourself to say that the rational soul that belongs to us moves accidentally, except in a metaphorical sense. This is because movement by accident (p. 182) is such that the thing has acquired a position and a place due to that in which it is found, and then that position and that place cease [to belong to it] due to its ceasing to be in that in which it was found, i.e., that in which it was imprinted.

CHAPTER 29. REMARK: THE FIRST CAUSED BEING IS AN INTELLECT IN THE CHAIN OF SEPARATE INTELLECTS (P. 183)

There are no two aspects to the unity of the First. It follows, as you have learned,[26] that the First is a principle only of something that is one and simple except perhaps by mediation.

As you have learned,[27] every body is composed of matter and form (p. 184). It must be clear to you then that the proximate principle of the existence of every body results from two [things] or from a principle involving two aspects so that it can produce two [things] simultaneously. For, [as] you have learned, neither matter nor form is a cause of the other absolutely, nor an intermediary absolutely. Rather, both need that which is a cause of each of them or of both of them together. They are not produced together without mediation from that which is indivisible. Therefore the first caused [being] is an intellect and not a body. The existence of a number of separate intellects had already been verified to you. There is no doubt that this first [being] that is created is in the chain of these intellects or in their intellectual location.

CHAPTER 30. ADMONITION: CONCERNING THE POSSIBILITY OF KNOWING THE MULTIPLICITY OF THE CELESTIAL BODIES, THE MULTIPLICITY OF THEIR MOVERS,[28] THE MULTIPLICITY OF THEIR PROPER OBJECTS OF DESIRE[29] AND THEIR ESSENTIAL DIFFERENCES (P. 185)

It is possible for you to know that the spheres and stars of the exalted spherical bodies are of a large number (p. 189). From the principles you have, you must know that for every one of these bodies—be it a sphere enveloping the earth, whether having a center that coincides with that of the earth or that lies outside it (p. 190) or a sphere not enveloping [the earth] such as epicycles or stars—(p. 191) there is a thing that is the principle of a circular motion around itself. In this the sphere is not distinguished from the stars (p. 192). The stars are transported around the earth due to the cause of the spheres in which they are fixed and not by penetrating the bodies of the spheres (p. 193). You will have additional insight into this if you reflect on the state of the moon, in its double movement and its two highest points, and the state of Mercury and its two highest points, and on the fact that if there were (p. 194) penetration, necessitated by the course of the stars or the course of the sphere in which [they] turn, this would not occur as such (p. 195). You know that all those bodies are the same with respect to the cause of movement [by] desire [for] resemblance. You know that it is not permissible to say what is sometimes said, namely, that the proper object of desire for the inferior bodies among them are those [bodies] that are superior to them (p. 196). You also know that their positions, movements, and places do not differ by nature except in that they do not belong to the same nature. Rather, they are different natures, even though, with respect to their relation to the natures of the [four] elements, they are united into one nature.

It remains for you to consider whether it is permissible that some of these bodies are proximate causes of the existence of some others or whether their causes are those separate substances. From here on, expect from us an expounding of this point.

CHAPTER 31. GUIDANCE: NO CELESTIAL BODY IS A CAUSE OF A BODY THAT IS INFERIOR TO IT OR THAT IT CONTAINS, NOR CAN THE CONTAINED BODY BE A CAUSE OF ITS CONTAINER (P. 197)

If you suppose a body that produces an action, that body produces this action only if the individual of that body becomes such a determined individual. If a celestial body were the cause of [another] celestial body contained in it, then, if you consider the state of the caused together with the existence of the cause, you will find this state in possibility (p. 198). As for the existence and necessity [of the effect], they are posterior to the existence and necessity of the cause. But the existence of the contained and the nonexistence of void in the container are simultaneous. Thus if we consider the individualization of the container as the cause the contained will be possible simultaneously with it. This is because the individualization of the cause is prior in existence and necessity to the individualization of the effect (p. 199). Therefore it is unavoidable that either the nonexistence of void [in the container] is necessary simultaneously with the necessity [of the existence of the container] (p. 200) or it is not. If it is, then the plenum of the contained is also necessary simultaneously with the necessity [of the existence of the container] (p. 201).[30] But it has been made clear that it is possible with the necessity of the container. If, on the other hand, it is not, then it is possible in itself and necessary through a cause (p. 202). Thus void is not impossible in itself but due to a cause. However, it has been shown that it is impossible in itself. It follows that no celestial [body] is a cause [of a body] that is inferior to it or that it contains.

As to whether the contained is a cause of that which is nobler, stronger, and greater than it, I mean the container, this is something that does not occur to any imagination, nor is it possible.

Chapter 32. Delusion and Admonition: Affirmation That the Containing and the Contained Bodies Are Simultaneously Necessary Through Two Other Things (p. 203)

Perhaps you will say: Suppose the cause of a celestial body is noncorporeal. Then it is necessary for you to say that from the noncorporeal a container and a contained follow—be they produced by one [thing] or by two (p. 204). It is unavoidable that the simultaneous possibility of void with the existence of the container may occur there as it occurs in what has been mentioned above. This is because you attribute to the container existence from a cause prior to the existence of the contained. Listen then.

You must know that the existence of the container accompanies the possibility of the contained only if the container is a cause prior to the contained. Hence the contained will have a possibility simultaneous with the existence of the container, since the existence of the container determines [its] surface. Hence what fills the container is not necessary simultaneously with the container if the former is an effect [of the latter]. Rather, it is necessary posterior to it (p. 205).

If, on the other hand, the container is not a cause, but is found simultaneously with the cause, then it is not necessary that the determination of its inferior surface be prior to the existence of the plenum in it, for this priority is not at all temporal (p. 206). Regarding essential [priority], it belongs only to a cause and not to that which is not a cause but is found simultaneously with a cause. Rather, we say that the container and the contained are simultaneously necessary from two things.

Chapter 33. Delusion and Admonition: Further Consideration of the Same Issue

Perhaps you will add saying that if from the principles already determined one can conclude that from an incorporeal thing a container comes into being, as well as another incorporeal thing from which the contained comes into being, then the necessity of the container and that of the other incorporeal thing are essentially simultaneous. But the contained is an effect of this other incorporeal thing. Therefore, if you consider its simultaneity (p. 207) with this other incorporeal thing, it will be possible. Hence, in that state in which the container is necessary, the contained is possible.

The answer to you is that, when determining the truth, this is [found to be] the first object of research. The answer to it is the same as that [answer].[31] The contained is possible only in accordance with its relation to the other incorporeal thing that is its cause. This relation does not suppose the possibility of void at all. Rather, this possibility is supposed by the determination of the interiority of the container. Further, the determination of the container has no priority over the contained. Not all that which is posterior is an effect—[the contained] is indeed posterior [to the container]. This is because, if priority and posteriority were in accordance with causation and with being cause [respectively], then where causation and being caused are absent there must not be priority and posteriority either. Also, since that which is found simultaneously with the cause is not necessarily a cause, that which is found simultaneously with that which is prior in causality is not necessarily prior except perhaps in time.

Chapter 34. Delusion and Admonition: The Container, the Contained, and the Determination of the Limit (p. 208)

Perhaps you will also say that, considered in themselves, both the container and the contained do not have necessary existence. Thus the void of their two places does not have necessary existence either. Listen then.

If these two are taken together as possible, then there will be no determination of anything, nor a place—if not filled. [Rather], there will be no void. What occurs occurs only if there is a determinant. It is necessary that, together with its determination, the limit either envelops a plenum or it does not envelop a plenum, in which case there will be void.

Chapter 35. Remark: The Assertion That the Containing Body Cannot Be the Cause of the Contained One Is True Whether "Cause" Is Used to Refer to the Form, the Soul or the Totality of the Containing Body

This statement is exactly the same, whether one attributes [causal] priority to the form of the containing body, to the soul of this body which is like its form, or to the totality of this body.

Chapter 36. A Follow-up: Inference to Be Drawn from the Preceding Evidence That Celestial Bodies Cannot Be Causes of Each Other (p. 209)[32]

It had been made clear that celestial bodies are not such that some of them are causes of some others. If you think to yourself, you will know that bodies act only by their forms (p. 210), and the forms that subsist in the bodies, and which are the perfections of those bodies,[33] produce their actions only by the mediation of that by virtue of which they subsist (p. 211). The body does not mediate between a [complete] thing and that which is not a body—be that matter or form—such that it makes both of them exist first, and then from both of them it makes the body exist (p. 212). Therefore corporeal forms are not causes either of the matters or of the forms of bodies (p. 213). But perhaps they prepare other bodies for the forms of what is renewed in them or for accidents.

CHAPTER 37. GUIDANCE AND LEARNING: CONCERNING THE UNITY OF THE NECESSARY INTELLECT, ITS PRODUCTION OF THE MULTIPLICITY OF POSSIBLE INTELLECTS THROUGH THE MEDIATION OF THE FIRST CAUSED INTELLECT, AND THE PRODUCTION OF THE MULTIPLICITY OF CELESTIAL BODIES THROUGH THE MEDIATION OF THESE INTELLECTS

It had been made clear to you that there exist incorporeal substances, and that that whose existence is necessary is just one only and does not share with anything else a genus or a species. Hence this multiplicity of incorporeal substances is caused (p. 214). You had also learned that the celestial bodies are effects of incorporeal causes; hence they are produced by this multiplicity. Further, you had learned that it is not permissible that that whose existence is necessary be a principle for two [things] together except by the mediation of one of them, nor a principle for a body except by mediation. Therefore it must be the case that the first effect of that whose existence is necessary is among these intellectual substances and is one, that the other intellectual substances are produced by the mediation of this one, and that the celestial [bodies] are produced by the mediation of these intellectual [substances].

Chapter 38. Additional Learning: Concerning the Necessity of the Simultaneous Existence of the Celestial Bodies with the Enduring Continuity of the Separate Intellects That Proceed from the First Principle

It is not permissible that the intellectual [substances] be arranged—as they are arranged—and that a corporeal body be necessitated by the last substances among them. This is because for every celestial body there is an intellectual principle (p. 215); a celestial body is not produced by the mediation of a celestial body. Thus it is necessary that the celestial bodies begin existing simultaneously with the enduring continuity of the intellectual substances, inasmuch as the existence of these substances necessarily descends in the acquisition of existence along the line of descent of the celestial bodies.

Chapter 39. Additional Learning: The Manner in Which Multiplicity Proceeds from the First Principle (p. 216)

Therefore it is necessary that there be an intellectual substance, from which an intellectual substance and a celestial body necessarily follow. It is known that the two necessarily follow from one, only under two aspects (p. 217). It is impossible for the First Principle to have a multiplicity of perspectives and manners because it is one in every respect, over and above different aspects and multiple perspectives, as has already been mentioned (p. 218). But this is not impossible in its effects. Therefore it is impossible that more than one comes from it (p. 219). But it is possible that [more than one] comes from its effects.[34] However, there are not two different aspects except those that belong to every one of these effects (p. 220), namely that every one of these effects is in itself possible in existence, and in the First necessary in existence (p. 221), and that it knows its essence and knows the First (p. 222). From the point of view of its knowing the First whose existence is necessary [it is a principle for something], from the point of view of its [know-ing] its state as related to the First, it is a principle for something else, and from the point of view of its [knowing] its essence, it is a principle for another thing still (p. 223). Since it is an effect [of the First], there is nothing that prevents it from being constituted of different things. Why not, since it has a possible quiddity and an existence that is neces-sary through another? Of these two the formal thing is a principle for a formal being (p. 224), and the thing that resembles matter is a principle for a being that befits matter (p. 225). Therefore, inasmuch as it knows the First that gives it its necessity, it is a principle for an intellectual substance (p. 226) and, [inasmuch as it knows] the other, it is a prin-ciple for a corporeal substance (p. 227). It is permissible for the latter to branch out into two things, by virtue of which it becomes a cause of a corporeal form and of a corporeal matter.

CHAPTER 40. DELUSION AND ADMONITION: THE DIVERSITY THAT IS IN THE ESSENCE OF EVERY INTELLECT DOES NOT NECESSITATE DIVERSE EXISTENCE IN AN INFINITE CHAIN (P. 228)

It is not the case that, if we say there is no diversity except from a diver-sity, the converse of this will necessarily be true, so that the diversity that is in the essence of every intellect will necessitate diverse exis-tence in an infinite chain, for you know that the affirmative is not converted universally.

CHAPTER 41. REMINDER: RECAPITULATION OF THE IMMEDIATE CREATION OF THE FIRST CAUSED INTELLECT AND THE MEDIATED CREATION OF THE OTHER CELESTIAL INTELLECTS AND BODIES (P. 229)

Thus the First creates an intellectual substance that is in truth created and, by the mediation of this substance, creates another substance and a celestial body (p. 230). The same is created from the [latter] intellectual substance. [This goes on] until the celestial bodies are completed. This leads to an intellectual substance from which no celestial body necessarily follows.[35]

CHAPTER 42. REMARK: CONCERNING THE EMANATION OF THE CELESTIAL WORLD INTO THE REGION OF GENERATION AND CORRUPTION (P. 231)

Therefore it must be the case that the matter of the world of elements necessarily comes from the last intellect. Nothing prevents the celestial bodies from aiding this in some way (p. 232). However, this is not sufficient for stabilizing the necessary flow of matter unless the form is joined to the matter (p. 233). As for the forms, they too emanate from that intellect. But their matters differ in accordance with their different merits for form—these merits being in accordance with their different preparations (p. 234). There is no principle for their differences other than the celestial bodies, by virtue of separating what surrounds the central region from what surrounds the enveloping region, and of dispositions whose details are much too sensitive to be grasped by [human] minds (p. 235), even though such minds discern their generalities. There the forms of the elements are found (p. 236). In them, and in accordance with their relations, which are due to the celestial bodies and to things that proceed from the celestial bodies, mixtures with different preparations for the powers for which they prepare are necessitated. There the plant souls (p. 237), the animal souls, and the rational souls emanate from the intellectual substance that neighbors this world (p. 238). With the rational soul the hierarchy of the existence of the intellectual substances ceases. For its perfection the rational soul is in need of bodily instruments and of the exalted emanation neighboring it (p. 239).

Even though we present this summary by way of exactitude, your reflection on (p. 240) the principles that have been given to you will guide you on the path of determining them by way of demonstration.

On Abstraction[1]

CHAPTER 1. ADMONITION: CONCERNING THE FLOW OF EXISTENCE FROM THE NOBLEST TO THE BASEST AND ITS RETURN TO THE SOURCE

Reflect on how existence began [descending] from what is noblest to what is [less] noble, until it ended in matter (p. 242). After that it returned [upward] from what is basest to what is [less] base, and [from there it moved from] the noble to the nobler,[2] until it reached the rational soul and the acquired intellect.[3]

Since the rational soul, which is a certain subject for the intelligible forms (p. 243), is not imprinted in the body in which it subsists, but only possesses an instrument through that body, the change of the body by death—due to which the body is no longer an instrument for the rational soul and a preserver of the relationship with it—does not harm the soul's substance. Rather its substance endures inasmuch as it receives existence from the enduring substances.

CHAPTER 2. INSIGHT: THE LOSS OF BODILY INSTRUMENTS DOES NOT HARM THE RATIONAL SOUL'S INTELLECTION (P. 244)

If the rational soul acquires the fixed habit of conjunction with the agent intellect, the loss of the instruments will not harm it. This is because it knows by itself, as you have already learned,[4] and not by its instruments. If it knows by its instruments, then no fatigue at all can occur to [any of its] instruments (as it unavoidably occurs to the sensitive and locomotive powers) without occurring also to the rational power (p. 245). But such fatigue does not occur [to the rational power]. Rather, it is often the case that the sensitive and locomotive powers are on the way to disintegration, while the rational power is either stable (p. 246) or on the way to growth and plentifulness. [Further], it is not the case that if fatigue occurs to the rational power at the same time that its instruments are fatigued, it is necessary, therefore, that the rational power does not act by itself. This is because, [as] you have learned,[5] the repetition[6] of the consequent itself does not yield a conclusion (p. 247).

I clarify this for you further by saying that something from without may occur to a thing and distract it from its acts by itself. But this does not show that the latter thing has no acts by itself (p. 248). However, if this thing exists, [if] it is not distracted by something else, and [if] it has no need for something else, then this shows that it has acts by itself.

CHAPTER 3. ADDITIONAL INSIGHT: POWERS THAT DEPEND ON THE BODY ARE FATIGUED BY BODILY ACTS, BUT THIS MAY OFTEN BE CONTRARY TO RATIONAL POWERS (P. 249)

Reflect also that the powers that subsist by bodies are fatigued by the repetition of acts, especially strong ones, in particular, if an act follows another immediately (p. 250). In such a case the weak is unnoticed, as is a weak odor after a strong one. The acts of the rational power may often be the opposite of what has been described [above].[7]

CHAPTER 4. ADDITIONAL INSIGHT: CONCERNING THE DIFFERENCE BETWEEN THE MODE OF APPREHENSION OF THE SENSITIVE POWERS AND THAT OF THE RATIONAL ONES (P. 251)

That whose act is by means of an instrument and has no proper act does not act concerning the instrument. That is why the sensitive powers do not in any way apprehend their instruments and do not in any way apprehend the apprehensions of their instruments. This is so because these powers have no other instruments [for apprehending] their instruments and the apprehensions of those instruments (p. 252), and they do not act except by means of instruments.

The rational powers, on the other hand, are not such, for they know everything.[8]

Chapter 5. Additional Insight: Further Clarification of the Independence of the Rational Soul in Its Intellection (p. 253)

If the rational power were imprinted in a body, be that the heart or the brain (p. 254), it would have perpetual knowledge of that body or no knowledge of it at all. This is because it knows only by virtue of its acquiring the form of the known object (p. 255). Thus, if it begins to have knowledge after not having it, it then acquires the form of the known object after not having this form. Because this power is material, it is necessary that what it acquires, such as the form of the known object that comes from the matter of this object, also exist in its matter (p. 256). Because the acquisition [of the form] of the known object is renewed, it is other than the form, which has not ceased numerically to be for it in its matter and for its matter (p. 257). Thus two forms for one thing would be acquired simultaneously in one matter, which is enveloped by the accidents of its individuals. But the falsehood of this has already been demonstrated (p. 258). Hence the form by virtue of which the rational power becomes intellective of its instruments is the form of the thing in which the rational power is found (p. 259) and [by virtue of which] this power is always joined to its instruments. This joining either necessitates constant knowledge (p. 260) or is not at all susceptible to knowledge. But neither of these two cases is true.

CHAPTER 6. CONTINUATION OF THESE REMARKS: THE ESSENTIAL PERFECTIONS OF THE RATIONAL SOUL (THE INTELLIGIBLES IT ACQUIRES INDEPENDENTLY) ENSURE ITS INCORRUPTIBILITY (P. 261)

Thus, you must know from this[9] that it belongs to the rational substance in us to know in itself.[10] Because it is a fundamental principle, it cannot be composed of a power receptive to corruption and [also] joined to the power of stability (p. 262).[11] If it is taken not as a fundamental principle but as a composite of something like matter and something like form, we fall back in discourse on a fundamental principle formed of two of its parts.[12]

[Because] the existence of accidents is in their subjects, therefore the capacity for their corruption and coming into existence is in their subjects. Hence no composition is formed in their subject, [if the subjects under consideration are fundamental principles, as is the rational substance] (p. 263).[13] If this is so, things similar to these subjects are not in themselves (p. 264) receptive to corruption after having been necessitated and stabilized by their causes.

CHAPTER 7. DELUSION AND ADMONITION: REFUTATION OF AN ANCIENT VIEW CONCERNING THE MANNER IN WHICH THE RATIONAL SOUL IS CHARACTERIZED BY ITS INTELLIGIBLES (P. 267)

A group of predecessors[14] believe that if any intellective substance knows an intelligible form it becomes the same as this form.[15]

But let us suppose that the intellective substance knows A and is, as they say, itself the known object of A; is it then, as it was when it did not know A, or has that [aspect] of it ended? If it is, as it was, then it will be the same whether (p. 268) or not it knows A. If, on the other hand, that [aspect] of it has ended, has it ended inasmuch as it is a state of it or inasmuch as it is its essence? If [it has ended] inasmuch as it is a state of it, while the essence endures, then, similar to the remaining changes, it is not as they say. If, on the other hand, [it has ended] inasmuch as it is its essence, then its essence would end and something else would come into existence—not that it itself becomes something else. If you also reflect on this, you will know that it requires a common matter and a composite, not a simple, renewal.

CHAPTER 8. ADDITIONAL ADMONITION: ANOTHER ARGUMENT IN SUPPORT OF THE ABOVE REFUTATION (P. 269)

Again, if this intellective substance knows A, and then knows B, would it be as it was when it knew A, so that it would be the same whether or not it knew B? Or would it become something else from which what has already been mentioned necessarily follows?

CHAPTER 9. ANOTHER DELUSION AND ADMONITION: FALSEHOOD OF ASSUMING THAT THE RATIONAL SOUL BECOMES ONE WITH THE AGENT INTELLECT WHEN IT INTELLECTS A THING ON THE GROUND THAT IT BECOMES ONE WITH THE ACQUIRED INTELLECT (P. 270)

They may also say that if the rational soul knows a thing it knows it only by its conjunction with the agent intellect. This is true. [But] they say that its conjunction with the agent intellect makes it become itself the same as the agent intellect. This is because it becomes the acquired intellect, and the agent intellect itself is joined to the soul which then becomes the acquired intellect.

It is evident that these people hold that the agent intellect is divisible, having one part rather than another (p. 271) joined [to the rational soul], or they hold that there is one conjunction for it, which renders the soul perfect and attaining all the intelligibles. [But] the impossibility of their view is that the rational soul is [considered by them] the acquired intellect, while this intellect's conceptions are independent.

Chapter 10. Anecdote: Concerning Porphyry's "Bad Ideas" on the Intellect and Intelligibles

To them belonged a man known as Porphyry.[16] He composed a book on the intellect and the intelligibles. This book is praised by the Peripatetics, yet it is full of bad ideas.[17] They themselves know that they do not understand it, nor does Porphyry himself [understand it either]. A man of his time contradicted him, and he contradicted that contradictor with what is more inferior than [the arguments of] the former.

Chapter 11. Remark: On the Meaning of a Thing Becoming Another (p. 272)

You must know that the statement of him who says "A thing becomes another thing not by way of change from one state to another and not by way of composition with another thing so that a third would be produced from these two; rather inasmuch as it was one thing and then became another" is an unintelligible poetic statement (p. 273). If each of the two things exists [after the union], then they are two distinct things.[18] If one of them is nonexistent, and if the nonexistent is that which was before [the union]—whether or not another thing comes into existence [after its nonexistence]—then it is impossible to assume that it is a second thing and the cause of its being (p. 274). If, on the other hand, both things are nonexistent, then neither of them can become the other. Rather, it would only be permissible to say that water becomes air inasmuch as the subject of the quality of water stripped itself of the quality of water and put on the quality of air or the like.

Chapter 12. A Follow-up: A Knower Is an Existing Essence in Which Intelligibles Are Established as a Thing Is Established in Another (p. 275)

Thus, it becomes apparent to you from this that whatever knows [anything] is an existing essence in which the intelligibles[19] are established in the manner in which a thing is established in another.

Chapter 13. Admonition: The Manner in Which the Intelligibles Are Represented in That Which Is Necessary in Existence and in the Principles That Follow It

It is permissible that in some manner the intelligible forms are acquired from external forms (p. 276) as, for example, the form of the sky is acquired from the sky. It is also permissible that the form first proceeds to the intellective power and then exists externally, as when you intellect a figure and then you make it exist.

It must be the case that that whose existence is necessary intellects the whole in the second manner.

Chapter 14. Admonition: Knowledge of That Whose Existence Is Necessary Is Due to This Intellectual Principle Itself; Otherwise There Would Be an Infinity of Separate Intellects

It is permissible that each of the two ways [of knowledge] occurs due to an intellectual cause, which conceives (p. 277) that whose form exists concretely or that whose form does not yet exist [concretely] in a substance receptive to the intelligible form. It is also permissible that this belongs to the intellectual substance due to itself, not to something else. Were it not for this, there would be an infinity of separate intellects. This must belong to that whose existence is necessary due to itself.

CHAPTER 15. REMARK: THE MANNER IN WHICH THAT WHOSE EXISTENCE IS NECESSARY KNOWS ITSELF AND KNOWS OTHER THINGS (P. 278)

That whose existence is necessary must know his essence by his essence, as has been already determined.[20] He knows what is posterior to him inasmuch as he is its cause and the source of its existence. Finally, he knows the remaining things inasmuch as they are necessitated in the chain of order that descends from him lengthwise and crosswise.

CHAPTER 16. REMARK: THE LEVELS OF REALIZATION IN THE UNIVERSE, THEIR OBJECTS AND QUALITY (P. 279)

The First's realization of things by his essence and in his essence is the best manner in which a thing can realize and in which a thing can be realized. This [realization] is followed [in the rank of goodness] by the necessary intellectual substances'[21] realization of the First owing to his illumination (p. 280) and of what is posterior to him and produced by his essence. After these two [realizations] come the realizations of the souls—these [realizations] being impressions and sketches from intellectual natures with different principles and relations.

CHAPTER 17. DELUSION AND ADMONITION: KNOWLEDGE OF THE MULTIPLICITY BY THAT WHOSE EXISTENCE IS NECESSARY DOES NOT DESTROY HIS UNITY (P. 281)

Perhaps you will say that if the intelligibles do not unite with that which knows [them] (p. 282), nor do some of them unite with each other (for the reason you had mentioned [above]),[22] and you had admitted that that whose existence is necessary knows everything (p. 283), then he is not truly one, but a multiplicity.[23]

We say that since his knowledge of his essence is by his essence, and [since] his subsisting as an intellect by himself due to his essence necessarily leads to his knowledge of the multiplicity (p. 284), the multiplicity comes as a necessary consequence posterior to and not included in the essence as a constituent of it. Further, the multiplicity proceeds in a hierarchy. The multiplicity of concomitants due to the essence—be they separate or nonseparate—do not cause a breach in the unity (p. 285). A multiplicity of relative and nonrelative concomitants as well as a multiplicity of negations occur to the First. This causes a multiplicity of names [for him], but it does not affect the unity of his essence.

Chapter 18. Remark: The Universal and Particular Manners in Which Particular Things May Be Known (p. 286)[24]

Particular things may be known as universal things are known, i.e., inasmuch as they are necessitated by their causes, as they are attributed to a principle whose species is individuated in its particulars. This is exemplified by the particular eclipse; for the occurrence of such an eclipse may be known due to the availability of its particular causes, the intellect's complete knowledge of these causes, and their being known as universals are known (p. 287). This is other than the temporal particular realization that judges that such an eclipse occurs now, that it occurred before, or that it will occur later. Rather, it is similar to knowing that a particular eclipse occurs when the moon reaches—this reaching being a certain particular [event], at such and such a time, this time being a certain particular [time]—such an opposition. But perhaps this eclipse occurred without the First Knower having full knowledge that it has occurred or that it has not occurred (p. 288), even though he knows it in the former manner. This is because the latter manner is another [kind of] particular realization that occurs with the occurrence of the realized object and is removed with its removal.

The former [manner of realization, however], is fixed for all times, even though it is knowledge of a particular. It is such that the knower knows that between the moon's being in such and such a place and its being in another there is a specific eclipse at a determined moment of the time [of its being at] the beginning of [one of the] two states (p. 289). The knower's knowledge of this is a fixed matter before the occurrence of the eclipse, with it, and after it.

CHAPTER 19. ADMONITION AND REMARK: TYPES OF ATTRIBUTE CHANGES OF WHICH ONLY THAT WHICH DOES NOT AFFECT THE ESSENCE MAY APPLY TO THAT WHICH IS NECESSARY IN EXISTENCE (P. 290)

The attributes of things may change in different ways of which [the following will be enumerated]:

[1 When] that which is white, for example, becomes black due to the change of a nonrelative, fixed attribute.

[2 When] a thing, for example, has the power to move a certain body (p. 291), but if that body becomes nonexistent then one can no longer say that that thing has the power to move that body. Therefore that thing no longer has its attribute, yet without a change in its essence, but in its relation. Its having power is an attribute of it which is one and followed in a primary and an essential manner by a relation to a universal thing, such as moving bodies in a certain state, for example. Zayd, Amr, stone, and tree are also included in this [relation], but in a secondary [and accidental] manner (p. 292). Its having power is not dependent on the individual relations in some unavoidable manner.[25] If Zayd were not at all in possibility, and the relation of power to move him did not occur at all, this would not harm [the mover's] power to move [things]. Thus [the mover's] primary possession of power is not changed by the change of the states of that which is one of the things over which the power is exercised. Rather, it is just the external relations that change only. This division is like the opposite of the above division.

[3 When] a thing, for example, knows that another thing is not, and then that that other thing comes into existence; the former thing then knows that the latter thing is. Hence the relation and the relative attribute change together (p. 293). Its having knowledge of a certain thing is something for which the relation is reserved, so that if it knows a universal concept this will not be sufficient for its having knowledge of the particular things one by one. Rather, knowledge of the conclusion is resumptive knowledge, necessitating a resumptive relation and a new disposition of the soul that has a new proper relation—this knowledge is other than knowledge of the premises and other than the disposition for the determination of their truth. This is not the same as its having power, i.e., its having different relations by one disposition.

Therefore, if [in the case of knowledge] the state of the object of the relation is made different by nonexisting or by existing, the state of the thing that has the attribute must become different not only in the relation of the attribute itself but also in the attribute that is necessarily followed by this relation.

Thus it is not permissible that that which is not subject to change undergo change (p. 294) either in accordance with the first division or in accordance with the third division. However, change in accordance with the second division is permissible in distant relations that have no influence over the essence.

CHAPTER 20. A SMALL POINT: THE DIFFERENCE BETWEEN A RELATIVE STATE AND A PURE ONE (P. 295)

Your being right or left is a pure relation.[26] However, your being capable or[27] knowing is being in a state stable in yourself and followed by a relation that is necessary or that [just] attaches. Thus, by being capable or knowing, you have a relative state and you do not have a pure state.

Chapter 21. A Follow-up: The Modality and Extent of the Knowledge That the Necessary in Existence Enjoys

Therefore the knowledge that that whose existence is necessary has of particular things must not be temporal knowledge such that it includes the present, the past, and the future (p. 296) in order that change of an attribute of its essence would occur. Rather, his knowledge of particular things must be in a manner holy and above duration and time (p. 297). He must know everything because everything is a necessary consequence of him—whether through an intermediary or without an intermediary. His destiny, which is the detailing of his first determination, leads in a necessary manner to [the existence of] everything individually, since,[28] as you have learned,[29] that which is not necessitated is not.

Chapter 22. Remark: Concerning Providence (p. 298)[30]

Providence is the First's knowledge of the whole and of how the whole must be so that it would have the best order (p. 299) and of the fact that it is necessarily derived from him and from his knowledge of it. Thus the existent corresponds to the known [which is] in the best order—without a motivating intention or quest from the First, the Truth.

Therefore the First's knowledge of the manner of the befitting arrangement of the existence of the whole is the source of the emanation of the good in the whole.[31]

Chapter 23. Remark: Addressing the Problem of Evil

Things that are possible in existence include [1] things whose existence can be primarily altogether free from evil, disorder, and corruption; [2] things that cannot give their advantages except if they are such that a certain evil proceeds from them at the jamming of motions and the clashing of movable things (p. 300). Further, in the division [of the things that are possible in existence, there are also] [3] things that are evil either absolutely or for the most part.

If the pure good is the principle of the emanation of the good and befitting existence, then the existence of the first division must necessarily emanate. This is exemplified by the existence of the intellectual substances and the like (p. 301). Also, the second division must necessarily emanate. This is because in the nonexistence of much good and in the nonproduction of it, as a precaution against [the presence of] slight evil, there is great evil. This is illustrated by the creation of fire; for fire would not give its advantages and would not complete its help in perfecting existence unless it is such that it harms and hurts whatever animal bodies happen to collide with it (p. 302). The same is true of animal bodies. They cannot have their advantages unless they are such that it is possible [A] for their states in their motions and rests, as is the case with the states of fire also, to lead to the coming together of clashes that harm; [B] for their states and the states of things in the world to lead to the occurrence of (p. 303) error from them[32] in the knotting of harm for the second life and for the truth; or [C] for an excess of an acting predominant agitation, such as desire or anger that harms the affairs of the second life (p. 304). The above-mentioned powers [such as fire] do not enjoy their richness unless they are such that accidental error and predominant agitation occur from them[33] on the occasion of clashes. This is so in individuals that are less [in number] than those who are safe and at times fewer than those of safety (p. 305).

Because this is known in the first providence, it is as if intended incidentally. Thus evil enters destiny incidentally, as if it were, for example, pleasing [to God] incidentally.

Chapter 24. Delusion and Admonition: Moral Evil Is Not Predominant (p. 306)

You may say that the majority of people are dominated by ignorance or obedience to desire and anger. Why then is this type [of evil] among them described as rare?[34] Listen then.

As the states of the body are in disposition three: [1] the state of the one who excels in beauty and health, [2] the state of the one who does not [excel] in these two [qualities] (p. 307), and [3] the state of [the one who suffers from] ugliness, illness, or chronic illness. The first and the second [types] receive an abundant or a moderate portion of worldly and physical happiness [respectively], or they are [simply] saved. Similarly, the states of the soul in its dispositions are three: [1] the state of the one who has attained the full virtue of mind and character. [one with this state] will have the highest degree of happiness in the future life (p. 308). [2] The state of the one who has not attained this [level], especially in [those virtues concerning] the intelligibles, yet one's ignorance is not an impediment to the second life, even though one does not have a large storage of knowledge that has great usefulness for the second life. Nevertheless, this person is among those who are in safety and who receive a portion of the goods of the future life. [3] Another one who, like the ill or the chronically ill, is subject to harm in the second life. Each one of the two extremes is rare. The middle is prevalent and predominant. If the virtuous extreme is added to the middle, [the number] of people saved becomes abundantly predominant.

Chapter 25. Admonition: Concerning Happiness in the Life to Come (p. 309)

Do not think that happiness in the future life is of one kind and do not think that happiness is not received at all except by perfecting [oneself] with knowledge, even though that makes the kind of this happiness noblest. Further, do not think that the various sins affect the certainty of salvation. Rather, that which creates eternal destruction is only a kind of ignorance (p. 310). That which exposes [people] to limited suffering is only a kind of vice and a certain degree of it. [However], this [happens] to a minority of individual human beings.

Do not listen to the one who considers salvation limited to a certain number of people and denied to the ignorant and sinful to eternity—God's mercy is plentiful.[35] About this [point] you will hear further explanation.

CHAPTER 26. DELUSION AND ADMONITION: THE REASON WHY THE REGION OF THE WORLD THAT HAS EVIL CANNOT BE FREE FROM EVIL

Or perhaps you will say: Was it not possible that the second division [of things possible in existence] might have been free from attachment to evil? The answer is: If it had been free from attachment to evil, it would have been something other than this division. But[36] the first division had already been freed from[37] evil. This division[38] is in its basic construction only among those things to which the great good cannot attach unless it is such that evil attaches to it by necessity at the occurrence of clashes. Thus, if it were free from this [evil], it would have been made other than itself—hence it is as if fire were made other than fire, and water other than water. Leaving out the existence of this division, as previously described,[39] does not befit the Good, as we have shown.[40]

CHAPTER 27: DELUSION AND ADMONITION: ADDRESSING THE PROBLEM OF DESTINY (P. 311)

Perhaps you will also say: If there is destiny, then why is there punishment? Reflect on the answer.

Punishment of the soul for its sin is, as you shall know, similar to the disease of the body for its gluttony. Thus it is one of the necessary consequences to which past conditions lead—these conditions together with their consequences are inescapable. As for the punishment that falls in another class,[41] which has[42] its principle from without,[43] that is another story (p. 312). Further, if a punisher from without is accepted, that is also good. This is because it is necessary that fear be present among the causes that are confirmed and hence useful in general. Belief [in such punishment] ensures fear.

Thus, [even] if it happens that, due to destiny,[44] one person transgresses the required fear and consideration, and so does wrong and commits a crime, [still,] belief [in an external punisher] was made to exist for the sake of the general good,[45] (p. 313) even though it is not suitable to that person and not required by the Choice Maker and the Merciful.

If there is nothing other than the person afflicted by destiny, there would not be much general and universal utility in his particular corruption. For the sake of the universal, attention should not be paid from the point of view of the particular. Similarly, for the sake of the whole, attention should not be paid from the point of view of the part. Thus an organ that hurts is severed in order that the body as a whole be saved.

As for the discourse about injustice and justice that has reached [us] and the discourse about acts said to be unjust (p. 314) and acts contrary to them and about the necessity of abandoning the former acts and adopting the latter—on the assumption that these are primary premises—they are not of universal necessity. Rather, most of them are among the widely accepted premises agreed upon for the sake of [self]-interest (p. 315). Perhaps there is among these [widely accepted] premises what can be demonstrated as sound with respect to some agents.

If the truths are determined, attention must then be paid to the obligations without their contraries.[46] You have learned the [various] types of premises in their places.[47]

Notes

ANALYSIS OF THE TEXT

1. *Remarks and Admonitions: Part One*, p. 46.

2. Ibid.

3. *Al-Ishārāt, Part Two*, p. 147.

4. *Ibn Sina and Mysticism*, p. 107.

5. *Al-Shifāʾ, al-Manṭiq, al-Madkhal*, pp. 12, 14.

6. Ibid., p. 14. For the division of the sciences, see also *al-Shifāʾ, al-Ilāhiyyāt*, bk. 1, ch. 1, pp. 3–4; *Manṭiq al-Mashriqiyyīn*, pp. 6–7; and *ʿUyūn al-Ḥikma*, p. 17.

7. *Al-Shifāʾ, al-Manṭiq, al-Madkhal*, p. 14.

8. *Al-Ishārāt*, pp. 192–93.

9. Ibid., pp. 208–9.

10. Ibid., pp. 212–13. Similitude in quantity and shape would be necessary as a result of the similitude found in pure matter, if pure matter were the only determining factor. But similitude in quantity and shape is not necessary. The conclusion to be drawn is that there are other factors in addition to matter responsible for the lack of similitude or the presence of difference in quantity and shape.

11. Ibid., p. 213.

12. Compare with al-Farabi, *Arāʾ Ahl al-Madīna al-Fāḍila*, pp. 76, 79.

13. *Al-Ishārāt, Part Two*, p. 229.

14. The idea of the relation of body to surface and surface to line minus line to point is basically Aristotelian, used to demonstrate the unique completeness of body among magnitudes. See Aristotle, *On the Heavens*, in *The Complete Works of Aristotle*, bk. 1, ch. 1: "A magnitude if divisible one way is a line, if two ways a surface, and if three a body. Beyond these there is no other magnitude,

because the three dimensions are all that there are, and that which is divisible in three directions is divisible in all. For, as the Pythagoreans say, the universe and all that is in it is determined by the number three, since beginning and middle and end give the number of the universe, and the number they give is the triad" (268 a 8–13). "Therefore, since 'every' and 'all' and 'complete' do not differ from one another in respect of form, but only, if at all, in their matter and in that to which they are applied, body alone among magnitudes can be complete. for it alone is determined by the three dimensions, that is, is an 'all'" (268 a 20–23).

15. See Aristotle, *Physics*, in *On the Heavens*, bk. 4.

16. *Al-Ishārāt, Part Two*, p. 250.

17. For a discussion of Ibn Sina's view on directions, see al-Tusi, *Commentary* (published with the edition of *al-Ishārāt, Part Two* used here), pp. 257–59.

18. For further information about the enveloping sphere, see Second Class, chs. 12–17.

19. Al-Tusi, *Commentary*, p. 262.

20. Ibid.

21. Ibid., pp. 262–63.

22. Ibid., p. 270.

23. For Ibn Sina's detailed discussion of directions, see *al-Shifā', aṭ-Ṭabī'iyyāt*, bk. 3, chs. 13–14, pp. 246–58.

24. *Al-Ishārāt, Part Two*, p. 278.

25. By "essential" is meant a universal element which is a constituent of the essence and without which the essence cannot be conceived and cannot be what it is. In other words, removing an essential element of an essence is removing the essence as it is. See *Remarks and Admonitions: Part One*, pp. 16–17, 53–55.

26. *Al-Ishārāt, Part Two*, p. 322.

27. Compare with Plato, *Timaeus*, in *The Collected Dialogues*, 29e.1–30a. 1–3, 30a.3–6. See also Plato's theory of creation in Shams Inati, *The Problem of Evil: Ibn Sina's Theodicy* (Binghamton: Global, 2000), pp. 18–20.

28. *Al-Ishārāt, Part Two*, pp. 340–42.

29. Al-Farabi, *Arā' Ahl al-Madīna al-Fāḍila*, p. 78.

30. By "intuition" is meant immediate knowledge, as chapter 11 of the Third Class asserts.

31. *Al-Ishārāt, Part Two*, pp. 344–45. For the soul's apprehension of itself independently of any bodily organs, see also *al-Shifā'al-Ṭabī'iyyāt, Part Two*, bk. 6, I, ch. 1, p. 13 and bk. 6, V, ch. 7, pp. 225–27.

32. *Al-Ishārāt, Part Two*, p. 356.

33. Ibid., p. 358.

34. Ibid., p. 359.

35. See, for example, al-Farabi, *Arāʾ Ahl al-Madīna al-Fāḍila,* where the only internal sense discussed is the imagination (*al-mutakhayyila*). This faculty is said to preserve the objects represented in the external senses after these senses no longer experience them. It is also described as a faculty that combines sensible objects with each other or separates them from each other (pp. 87, 100). What Ibn Sina calls the estimative faculty is briefly hinted at in *Arāʾ Ahl al-Madīna al-Fāḍila* and is not even given a specific name, but simply referred to as a sense (p. 91). Thus, the faculty of imagination in al-Farabi plays the role of three internal sense faculties in Ibn Sina: the common sense, which views the sense objects after the external senses no longer experience them; the representational faculty, which preserves the objects of the common sense; and the imagination, which, among other things, combines and separates the sense objects.

36. *Al-Ishārāt, Part Two,* pp. 377–78.

37. See Third Class, note 16.

38. *Al-Ishārāt, Part Two,* p. 395. In *Fī al-ʿAhd,* Ibn Sina contrasts intuition with unintelligibility or failure to understand (*al-ghabāwa*). *Fī al-ʿAhd,* in *Tisʿ Rasāʾ il fī al-Ḥikma wal-Ṭabīʿ iyyāt,* ed. Hasan Asi (Cairo: Dār Qābis, 1986), p. 119.

39. *Al-Ishārāt, Part Two,* p. 394.

40. For further information about Ibn Sina's concept of the agent intellect, its nature, and its function, see *Al-Najāt, al-Ṭabīʿ iyyāt,* bk. 6, p. 231.

41. *Al-Ishārāt, Part Two,* p. 403.

42. Ibid., pp. 406–8.

43. Compare with al-Farabi, *Arāʾ Ahl al-Madīna al-Fāḍila,* pp. 46–47.

44. *Al-Ishārāt, Part Two,* pp. 449–50.

45. *Al-Shifāʾ, al-Ilāhiyyāt,* bk. 1, ch. 1, p. 5.

46. Ibid., p. 17.

47. *Al-Najāt, al-Ilāhiyyāt,* bk. 1, p. 235; *ʿUyūn al-Ḥikma,* p. 47.

48. See al-Tusi, *Commentary to al-Ishārāt, Part Three,* p. 14.

49. Ibid., p. 19.

50. Ibid., p. 20. For the meaning of "necessary in existence" and "possible in existence," see also *Al-Mabdaʿ wal-Maʿād,* pp. 2–4.

51. *Al-Ishārāt, Part Three,* p. 21.

52. Ibid., pp. 31–32.

53. Ibid., pp. 33–34.

54. Which is impossible.

55. *Al-Ishārāt, Part Three,* pp. 45–46.

56. Ibid., p. 49.

57. *Al-Shifāʾ, al-Ilāhiyyāt,* bk. 8, ch. 4, p. 347.

58. Ibid. An example of genus is "animality" for "human being." For further information about the concept of genus, see *Remarks and Admonitions: Part One,* pp. 17–18, 19–20, 58*n*41, 59–60, 64–66, 69.

59. Species is exemplified by "human being." For elaboration on the concept of species, see *Remarks and Admonitions: Part One,* pp. 17–18, 19–20, 60*n*49, 61*n*50, 62*n*55, 64–66, 70.

60. "Rationality" for "human being" is an example of the difference. See *Remarks and Admonitions: Part One,* pp. 17–18, 19–20, 41, 65–66, 69.

61. The definition is given and discussed in *Remarks and Admonitions: Part One,* pp. 19–21, 40–41, 49, 70–72.

62. See *Al-Shifāʾ, al-Ilāhiyyāt,* bk. 8, ch.4, p. 348.

63. *Al-Ishārāt, Part Three,* pp. 52–53.

64. Ibid., p. 53.

65. Al-Razi considers this inquiry as a purely linguistic discussion. See al-Tusi, *Commentary, Al-Ishārāt, Part Three,* p. 61.

66. See ibid., p. 64.

67. See ibid., p. 66.

68. Compare with al-Najāt, *al-Ilāhiyyāt,* bk. 1, pp. 249–50.

69. See *Al-Ishārāt, Part Three,* pp. 77–78.

70. Ibid., pp. 90–93.

71. Ibid., p. 95.

72. Al-Tusi, *Commentary,* p. 95.

73. *Al-Ishārāt, Part Three,* pp. 128–29.

74. Ibid., pp. 118–19.

75. al-Najāt, *al-Ilāhiyyāt,* bk. 2, p. 305.

76. *Al-Ishārāt, Part Three,* p. 123.

77. The text here is problematic, as the word *yanbaghī* could mean "that must be" or "desired" (by another). Al-Tusi is of the opinion that Ibn Sina intends the latter (*Commentary,* p. 125). However, I am of the opinion that Ibn Sina intends the former. If al-Tusi's interpretation is correct, the desire of the object of generosity becomes an essential element of generosity, something that would lead to a strange use of "generosity." For example, if X desires to kill Y with a gun, and Z provides X with the gun without expecting any compensation, Z would be said to be "generous."

78. *Al-Ishārāt, Part Three,* pp. 125, 127.

79. Ibid., p. 124.

80. Ibid., p. 132.

81. Compare with Plotinus, *The Enneads,* II, 1, III, 2, ch. 1. See also Inati, *The Problem of Evil,* pp. 54–55.

82. *Al-Ishārāt, Part Two*, pp. 239–48.

83. Ibid., p. 245.

84. *Al-Ishārāt, Part Three*, pp. 134–35.

85. Ibid., p. 137.

86. As Aristotle believes.

87. *Al-Najāt, al-Ṭabīʿiyyāt*, bk. 3, p. 174.

88. Ibid., p. 175.

89. *Al-Ishārāt, Part Three*, pp. 179–80.

90. Plotinus, *Enneads*, vi, 4, ch. 4.

91. *Al-Ishārāt, Part Three*, pp. 209–13.

92. Ibid., pp. 229–30.

93. Ibid., pp. 234–35.

94. For Ibn Sina's proof that, though the soul occurs with the occurrence of the body, it does not die with its death, nor is it essentially subject to corruption, see al-Najāt, *al-Ṭabīʿiyyāt*, bk. 6, pp. 223–27.

95. Ibn Sina elaborates his view of the independence of the rational soul both in existence and in intellection in *Aḍḥawiyya fī al-Maʿād li-Ibn Sīna*, pp. 132–42.

96. *Al-Ishārāt, Part Three*, p. 246.

97. Ibid., pp. 247–48.

98. Ibid., p. 250.

99. Ibid., pp. 255–60.

100. *Al-Mabdaʾ wal-Maʿād*, pp. 6–10.

101. Ibid., p. 1.

102. *Al-Ishārāt, Part Three*, p. 275.

103. Ibid., p. 277.

104. By "necessary concomitants," Ibn Sina means nonconstitutive universals, which, like the essentials or constituents, are also elements without which the essence is inconceivable. He insists that, in addition to the constituents, there are elements that are necessary for the conception of the essence. These are the necessary concomitants (*Remarks and Admonitions: Part One*, p. 16). This does not mean that the removal of the necessary concomitants causes the removal of the essence, "but that their removal indicates that there is no essence to which they attach. If there is no "capacity for laughter," then there is no "human being." The removal of the essence itself is caused by one or more of its internal elements. Thus while necessary concomitants resemble the essentials in that the essence cannot be conceived without them, they differ in that the removal of the former indicates that the essence has been removed but the removal of the latter causes the removal of the essence" (ibid.).

105. *Al-Ishārāt, Part Three*, p. 285.

106. Al-Ghazali, *Tahāfut al-Falāsifa*, ed. Sulayman Dunya (Cairo: Dār al-maʿārif, 1972), pp. 345–47, 350–52.

107. Qur'an, 34, 3.

108. *Al-Ishārāt, Part Three*, p. 290.

109. See, for example, *al-Shifāʾ, Metaphysics*, p. 227.

110. *Al-Mabdaʾwal-Maʿād*, p. 90.

111. God is said to be "al-jūd al-maḥḍ" (the pure generosity; the pure good), *al-Ishārāt, Part Three*, p. 300.

112. Ibid., pp. 299–300.

113. Ibid., p. 301. See also *al-Shifāʾ, Metaphysics*, pp. 232–33.

114. Ibid., p. 229–30.

115. Ibid., p. 229.

116. For a detailed discussion of this point, see Inati, *The Problem of Evil*, pp. 74–75.

117. *Al-Shifāʾ, Metaphysics*, p. 236. In his translation of the passage Marmuura gives essentially the same reading:

Things in the [faculty of] estimation are either [a] things which, if [reckoned in the] estimation as existing, cannot but be absolutely evil; [b] things whose existence [consists] in being good, it being impossible for them to be evil and deficient; [c] things in which goodness predominates if their existence comes to be, anything but this being impossible for their natures; [d] things in which evilness predominates; or [e] things in which the two states are equal. Regarding that wherein there is no evilness, this has been found in the natures [of things]. As for that which is either entirely evil or in which evil predominates, or also where it equals [even the good], this never exists. As for that in whose existence the good predominates, it is the more appropriate [for it] to exist if what is predominate in it is its being good.

The Metaphysics of the Healing, pp. 345–46.

118. *Al-Ishārāt, Part Three*, p. 213.

119. Plato, *Laws*, 10.903b.5-c.1–6.

120. Aristotle, *Metaphysics*, Λ 1077a, 16–23.

121. For an interesting discussion of Leibniz's thought on the issue of the best possible world, see Murray, "Leibniz on the Problem of Evil."

122. *Al-Shifāʾ, Metaphysics*, pp. 230–31.

123. Ibid., p. 229.

124. Ibid.

125. Ibid., pp. 228–30.

126. It is worth noting here that in *al-Ishārāt* only the concept of punishment is discussed. However, because reward and punishment are contraries, it is easy to derive Ibn Sina's view of reward from his view of punishment. Also, the two concepts are discussed thoroughly in some of Ibn Sina's other works. See, for example, *al-Shifāʾ, al-Ilāhiyyāt*, bk. 9, ch. 7, pp. 423–32. That is why I included both concepts, as they both relate to destiny.

127. Averroes, *Averroes' Commentary on Plato's Republic*, vol. 1, xi, 5–7. See also Hourani, "Averroes on Good and Evil," 23.

128. *Al-Ishārāt, Part Three*, p. 311.

129. Ibid., pp. 311–12.

130. Plato, *Theaetetus*, in *The Collected Dialogues*, 176A, 5–8; Plotinus, *The Enneads*, III, 2, ch. 5.

FIRST CLASS

Al-namaṭ (manner, model, type, class). It has been translated here as "class," since every *namaṭ* is intended as a class of certain issues.

1. This is the "delusion" that Ibn Sina attributes to some people he does not name here. It is obvious, though, that the reference is to some ancient theorists of atomism. The delusion can be summed up as follows: (1) Parts are not bodies. (2) Parts are the constituents of bodies. (3) Parts are uncuttable or indivisible and as such, they cannot accept division in any way whether by fracture, cutting, imagination, or even hypothesis. (4) A part that falls in the middle of an organization prevents the two extremes from contact.

2. See Aristotle, *Physics*, VI, 1, 231, a 21–231 b 18.

3. The person intended here is probably the Muʿtazilite theologian Ibrahim al-Nazzam (d. 845; see al-Tusi, *Commentary, Part Two*, p. 158). For a short exposition of al-Nazzam's position on this matter, see McGinnis, "Arabic and Islamic Natural Philosophy."

4. That is, the kind mentioned in the previous chapter.

5. That is, as one and undivided.

6. Text: *wa* (and). It has been translated here as "or" to keep the distinction between division by imagination and division by hypothesis, made in chapter 1 of the present Class. If one fails to imagine division, one does not thereby necessarily fail to hypothesize it.

7. That is, divisible to infinity.

8. Recall that disjunction is one of the manners of division. Therefore it is superfluous to mention it after having mentioned division.

9. That is, the corporeal form.

10. This is the end of the delusion.

11. The species, according to Ibn Sina, is one of the five essential universals: genus (e.g., animality for human beings), species (e.g., humanity), difference
(e.g., rationality for human beings), property (e.g., laughter for human beings),
and common accident (e.g., blackness for crows). The essentiality of the species
is relative to the individuals subsumed under it, as it is a constituent of them.
In this it is similar to genus and difference in that their essentiality is relative
to the species inasmuch as they are constituents of it. *Remarks and Admonitions:
Part One*, p. 17.

12. That is, not in conception, for it can be conceived apart from shape.

13. That is, free from matter.

14. That is, due to matter and the place of matter.

15. Text: *Al-qābil* (the receptacle). Forget's reading (p. 96) *Al-ḥāmil* (the subject) is adopted here: *Kitāb al-Ishārāt wal-Tanbīhāt*. The reference is to matter.

16. That is, the specific form.

17. That is, the corporeal form.

18. That is, wholeness and individuality that occur to the sphere due to its
matter.

19. That is, the fact that the part is assumed to be posterior to the whole.

20. In other words, matter.

21. By which is meant the underlying support, i.e., matter.

22. The position of a thing is its being such that one can point to it sensibly.

23. That is, the specific forms.

24. That is, the matter.

25. Because matter is one. But the similitude in quantity and shape is actually
not necessary. The conclusion to be drawn is that there are other factors in addition to matter that determine or individuate the corporeal form.

26. Ibn Sina does not specify here what these external determinants and
states are. But, according to al-Tusi, "These determining factors are "the agent
causes—the celestial powers and the terrestrial states, which are the prior forms,
the natural changes, and the external forces. All of these are agent causes for the
individuation of the forms. [These agent causes are opposed to] matter, which is a
potential cause" (*Commentary, Part Two*, p. 213).

27. Among these secrets that al-Tusi points out are (1) the existence of an old
principle from which the individuation in matter occurs when matter is prepared
to receive such individuation, and (2) the existence of a body that has a permanent
continuous motion; in short, the causes that organize and regulate the universal
system (213).

28. That is, its subsistence not in conception, but as individuated in external existence.

29. By "unrestricted cause" is meant that which constitutes a cause by itself.

30. That is, 3 and 4.

31. According to al-Tusi, the secret intended here is that the cause of things is something separate, permanent, and other than matter, and from which the existence of matter overflows, not from it independently, but also by the additional help of the form. He asserts that the need of the matter for the form is demonstrated by the fact that it is impossible for matter to be free from the form, not as an individual form, but as a universal one, and that if the effect is one, as is matter, its cause must be one. Therefore, the cause of the existence of matter must also be one. Commentary, Part Two, p. 219.

32. That is, the specific forms.

33. Such as limit and shape.

34. Effects of existence and effects of quiddity.

35. Al-Razi is reported to have held that this statement is intended to refer to the following idea in the present chapter: "the things that are causes of the quiddity of the form or of the form's being in positive existence would also be prior to matter in existence." See al-Tusi, Commentary, Part Two, p. 227; also al-Shifā', al-Ilāhiyyāt, bk. 2, ch. 4.

36. Despite the lack of clarity, if not confusion, in part of the text of this chapter and al-Tusi's commentary on it, I believe that al-Tusi attributes to al-Razi the assertion that the following idea in the present chapter is intended: "The form, though, is an effect of a certain genus whose essence is inseparable from that of the cause." Al-Tusi, Commentary, Part Two, p. 227.

37. In other words, if a corporeal form cannot be except owing to or in association with limit and shape, and if limit and shape cannot be except owing to matter, it would follow that corporeal form cannot be except owing to matter or in association with it. But this is impossible, if it is assumed that corporeal form is prior to matter. The chapter closes with the conclusion that corporeal form is not prior to matter and, therefore, cannot be an independent cause or even an intermediary for it. (An intermediary for a thing must also be prior to that thing.)

38. Text: shay' (a thing), but "things" is more appropriate here, because what is intended is limit and shape.

39. Text: wa-lais bi-wājib an naqûl (it is not necessary that we say).

40. Text: aḥadihimā (one of them).

41. The category intended here is the third division listed in chapter 19 of the present class, according to which "the form is a partner with something else; on the basis of the union of both, matter subsists."

42. *Sabab aṣl* (a fundamental cause). Later, this will be called *ʿaql faʿʿāl* (agent intellect).

43. This determinant is the celestial circular motion.

44. That whose form is inseparable from it is the celestial sphere.

45. Goichon's reading of this is as follows: "En effet, l'impossible se meut parfois du noir au blanc et il n'y a pas de blanc après [in fact, the impossible sometimes changes from black to white, and there is no white afterward]"; Goichon, *Livre des directives et remarques*, p. 277. But this reading does not make any sense.

46. Text: *wa* (and).

SECOND CLASS

1. That is, the front and the back. Thus six directions are pointed out. Two are unchangeable and are referred to as "natural" (p. 261). These are upward and downward. The other four are changeable and are not natural. These are right and left, and front and back. For the purpose of his argument, proving that there is a simple spherical body that determines the directions, Ibn Sina takes up for discussion only the unchangeable natural directions.

2. Text: *mutashābih* (similar; uniform), by which Ibn Sina seems here to mean "infinite." The position of a direction cannot be determined by a void, whether infinite or finite. It is not possible in an infinite void, because the infinite has no limit, and it has been stated that a direction is a limit. Nor can it be determined in a finite void, since there is no such void, as has been made clear. A direction cannot be determined in an infinite plenum either, for an infinite plenum has no limit. It remains that the position of a direction is to be found in a finite body. This is the conclusion Ibn Sina seeks to reach.

3. Text: *khārijan ʿanh* (outside it). However, it is clear that what is intended is that the position of a direction lies outside the void and the infinite plenum. Thus "it" has been replaced by "them."

4. Text: *al-mayl* (propensity). For a definition of this term, see Jurjani, *Kitāb al-Taʿrīfāt*, p. 258; Goichon, *Livre des directives et remarques*, p. 284, note 2.

5. That is, the natural propensity.

6. That is, the degree of strength of the natural propensity of a body depends on the degree of strength of the external influence. The stronger this influence, the weaker the natural propensity and vice versa.

7. In other words, if the propensity of a body is the inclination to move toward the natural place of that body, and if the body is already in its natural place, that body will not have any propensity.

8. Text: *al-mayl al-qasriyy* (propensity by violence; by force) is contrasted with internal or natural propensity, as it is the inclination of a body to move owing to an external force.

9. That is, the time required by the second object.

10. That is, if we suppose that the first object takes five minutes to cross five miles, the second object eight minutes to cross five miles, and the third object eight minutes to cross eight miles. You see from this that the relation of the distance of the third object to the distance of the second object (eight to five) is the same as the relation of the time of the second object to the time of the first object (eight to five). You also see that the third and first objects take the same time to cross the same distance (eight to eight, which is the same as five to five).

11. This delusion involves a denial of the assertion made in chapter 6 of the present class.

12. In the sense that its essence has the potentiality for such a place.

13. *Istiḥqāqan.*

14. *Istiḥqāqan.*

15. This last sentence is based on Forget's reading, *Kitāb al-Ishārāt wa-al-tanbīhāt,* p. 111: "Al-makān muṭlaqan wa-in lam yakun ṭabiʿiyyan lā yanfakk ʿanh wa-in lam yakun isthqāqan muṭlaqan" (The place [of a body] is absolute, even though it is not natural and inseparable from the body in spite of the fact that it is not absolutely required [by the essence]). Dunya's reading seems corrupt here: *Al-makan muṭlaqan* (the place is absolute).

16. This is the end of the delusion.

17. *Istiḥqāq.*

18. *Istiḥqāq.*

19. That is, that is what is sought.

20. *Istiḥqāq.*

21. A linear change for such a body has already been ruled out (see chapter 4 of the present class.

22. Text: *mayl mustadīr* (a circular propensity).

23. Text: *al-mutaḥarrik* (the movable).

24. *Li-istiḥqāq.*

25. Text: *maylan mustaqīman* (a linear propensity). The phrase will be translated hereafter this way.

26. Text: *aw* (or). It is clear that the issue here is not a matter of either/or. The point is that while a body may be devoid of certain active powers, such as color, it cannot be devoid of some other active powers, such as heat, cold, or warmth. It is more appropriate, therefore, to read *aw* as *wa* (and), which can also be translated as "also," as it has been here.

27. That is, the celestial bodies.

28. That is, movements of the other elements: earth and fire.

29. That is, wipe them off as often as you please; still you find that they collect again on the container.

30. Text: *mutashābih* (cf. note 2 of the present class for the meaning of this word.) What is intended here is that the intermediacy they achieve is an average of the qualities of the parts.

31. Text: *al-ṣayyāḥa* (crying out or screaming). This is a reference to the explosion-like sound produced by such bottles if filled with water, completely sealed, and placed on a hot fire. Though no fiery particles enter them, the liquid in them becomes very hot and undergoes a qualitative change, contrary to the objector's view. See Goichon, *Livre des directives et remarques*, p. 299, note 2.

32. This is a highly combustible kind of wood.

33. Text: *bil-gharaḍ* (for the purpose). The species is whatever is composed of the four elements.

34. That is, the four elements.

THIRD CLASS

1. See chapter 11 of the present class for the definition of "intuition."

2. That is, without memory of anything.

3. *Idrāk* ("attainment," "realization," "grasping," "perception," "apprehension"). As I have argued in *Ibn Sina and Mysticism*, p. 71, Ibn Sina uses *idrāk* not "in the sense of mechanical reaching, grasping, or possessing of a thing" but in the sense of becoming aware of it. Therefore, translating this word as "perception" or "apprehension" would seem reasonable. I have translated it in this work as "apprehension" to avoid its being taken in the usual sense to refer only to "sense awareness, excluding rational or intellectual awareness" In other words, while aware of the other translation possibilities of this word, preference was given to "apprehension" to see to it that it is not necessarily taken to refer to mental interpretation of information received from the sense organs, since Ibn Sina uses the word not only in the sense of sensations but also in a more general sense to cover even the soul's direct knowledge of its existence.

4. That is, not only during the time in which you are suspended in free air with the members of your body not in contact, but also outside that time. However, the issue of with what the soul is apprehended prior and after the supposed suspension in free air is raised here but not addressed until chapters 4 and 5.

5. This chapter raises two questions: with what is the soul apprehended, and what is the nature of the soul that is apprehended? The first question is answered in this chapter, the second in the following chapter.

6. The reason is that it has been assumed above that your intellect and senses are not in a position in which they can perceive the soul. Therefore, they cannot operate as instruments or intermediaries for such perception.

7. I eliminated the following phrase from the text, as it seems unnecessary: "fa-innah lā wasaṭ" (thus, there is no intermediary). My reading corresponds to that of Forget, *Kitāb al-Ishārāt wal-tanbīhāt*, p. 119.

8. But that is impossible.

9. Such as the imagination.

10. See, for example, chapters 8 and 9 of the present class.

11. That is, more general than the situation in which you are suspended in free air with the members of your body not in contact.

12. Text: *yulmas* (touch). Dunya's edition has *yudrak* (apprehend), which is the accurate reading. *Al-Ishārāt, Part Two.*

13. It is curious as to why Ibn Sina chose to move directly to a discussion of the internal senses without any treatment of the external senses. It could be that he found it unnecessary, in a book of brief comments, to include a discussion on something whose existence is obvious to all, as is the existence of the external senses. For Ibn Sina's view on the external senses, see, for example, *Ibn Sina and Mysticism*, pp. 9, 47–48, 53–54, and 98–99.

14. The reference here is to the common sense in which the sensibles are collected and the representational faculty in which the objects of the common sense are stored, as will soon become clear.

15. Text: *al-bāligha* (that which has reached the objective; that which has matured; that which is of a high order).

16. In this chapter Ibn Sina uses the beautiful and famous Qur'anic metaphoric verse in Surat an-Nūr (Chapter on Light) to describe the powers of the theoretical intellect of the rational soul (Qur'an, XXIV, 35). In doing so, Ibn Sina may be said to have paved the way for later Muslim mystics, including al-Ghazali, Ibn Arabi, and Rumi, for giving this verse a mystical interpretation.

17. See Goichon, *Livre des directives et remarques,* p. 331, note 4.

18. By which is meant the habitual intellect.

19. This being the soul.

20. That is every genus, such as "animality," has the preparedness to receive its differences; a difference being that which distinguishes the species under a genus from each other. A difference is exemplified in "barking" for dog, "rationality" for human being, and "neighing" for horse.

21. Text: *ashadd nafsāniyya*.

22. That is, the object of the sensible volition is sensible.

23. That is, the object of the intellectual volition is intellectual.

24. The first body is the enveloping sphere.

25. This is an objection, according to which the search of the animal power for nourishment as such is universal, yet produces search for a particular nourishment. Thus the particular can arise from the universal. This objection is obviously directed against Ibn Sina's claim that what is universal cannot by itself produce what is particular.

26. Text: *yuʿqal* (known). Forget's reading (p. 137) *yufʿal* (done) seems here more fitting.

FOURTH CLASS

1. See Goichon, *Livre des directives et remarques*, p. 352, note 1.

2. Text: *wa* (and).

3. The idea that final causality has some causal priority over efficient causality is an Aristotelian concept more fully worked out in Ibn Sina. See Aristotle, *De Partibus Animalium*, 639b: "The causes concerned in the generation of the works of nature are, as we see, more than one. There is the final cause and there is the motor cause. Plainly, however, the cause is the first which we call the final one. For this is the Reason, and the Reason forms the starting-point, alike in works of art and in works of nature. For consider how the physician or builder sets about his work. He starts by forming for himself a definite picture . . . and this he holds forward as the reason and explaination of each subsequent step that he takes, and of his acting int his or that way as the case may be." *De Partibus Animalium*, trans. William Ogle, in *The Basic Works of Aristotle*, ed. Richard McKeon (New York: Random House, 1941).

4. As is well known, Ibn Sina's distinction between a thing's essence and its existence had a direct influence on Aquinas. See Thomas Aquinas, *De Ente et Essentia*, esp. ch. 4: "But every essence or quiddity can be understood without understanding anything about its existence: I can understand what a man is or what a phoenix is and nevertheless not know whether either has existence in reality. Therefore, it is clear that existence is something other than the essence or quiddity, unless perhaps there is something whose quiddity is its very own existence, and this thing must be one and primary." *De Ente et Essentia*, trans. Robert Miller, http://www.fordham.edu/halsall/basis/aquinas -esse.asp.

5. I.e., of both the form and the matter.

6. "Ibn Sina makes the distinction between necessary and possible existence fundamental in his metaphysics, following in the footsteps of Aristotle who
described his First Cause as necessarily existing. See Aristotle, *Metaphysica*, XII,
1072b: "The first mover, then, exists of necessity."

7. But this is impossible. A thing cannot cause itself.

8. Ibn Sina added the present sentence to draw attention to the fact that
whether *kull* is used in the sense of "all the units" or in the sense of "every one of
the units," this will not work.

9. As "rational" is a cause of "laughter."

10. Ibn Sina is confirming here that the necessary in itself cannot divide in
any sense. That means it cannot divide into matter and form, into species and
genus, or into similar parts.

11. This means that all things other than God derive their existence from
without.

12. See chapters 5 and 6 of the present class.

13. The reference here is to *Remarks and Admonitions, Part One,* pp. 54, 55–57,
62–63.

14. This is because whatever is a body or is dependent on a body is caused.

15. That is, if this sensible body is terrestrial.

16. That is, if this sensible body is celestial.

17. Text: *illā* (except).

18. In part 1 of *al-Ishārāt* it was pointed out that a definition requires both a
genus and a difference. Therefore no definition is possible for anything that does
not have these two universal qualities.

19. See Goichon, *Livre des directives et remarques,* p. 370, note 1.

20. Al-ʿirfān.

21. See the Third Class of this work.

22. Qur'an, XLI, 53.

23. Ibid.

FIFTH CLASS

This is a revised version of the Fifth Class, trans. Shams C. Inati in *An Anthology of Philosophy in Persia,* ed. Sayyed Hossein Nasr and Mehdi Aminrazavi (London:
Tauris, 2008), 1:269–76.

Al-ṣunʿ (creation ex nihilo). Ibn Sina intends by *al-ṣunʿ*, the act of bringing into
existence something that is preceded by nonexistence. See al-Tusi, *Commentary,* in

Al-Ishārāt wal-Tanbīhāt, Part Three, p. 485. *Al-ṣunʿ* is creation ex nihilo and is mediated. See chapter 9 of the present class.

Al-ibdāʿ (immediate creation). This is the act of bringing into existence something that is not preceded by nonexistence. See al-Tusi, *Commentary, Part Three*, p. 485. This is immediate creation. See chapter 9 of the present class.

1. In *al-Najāt*, Ibn Sina attributes this view specifically to *al-mutakallimūn* (the theologians). *Al-Najāt, al-Ilāhiyyāt*, bk. 1, p. 249.

2. In other words, is it the case that existence that depends on something else depends on it because that existence is possible in itself and necessary through another, or because it is something that comes into existence after nonexistence?

3. That is, of being necessary through another.

4. Text: *fī kull shayʾ* (in everything), that is, in every case.

5. Text: *lam yabʿd* (it is not farfetched), but a stronger claim must be made here. It is not only not farfetched but also necessary.

6. That is, the possibility of existence and the possibility of nonexistence.

7. To Ibn Sina, emanation from the One is necessary, as it was to Plotinus. See *Enneads*, III.2.3: "The world, we must reflect, is a product of Necessity, not of deliberate purpose: it is due to a higher Kind engendering in its own likeness by a natural process."

8. *Bil-tafrīq*.

9. Ibn Sina follows Plotinus in that the One can only produce one thing. But Ibn Sina's use of necessary and possible existence to explain further emanations makes his view distinctive. See Plotinus, *Enneads*, V.6: "The mind demands the existence of these Beings, but it is still in trouble over the problem endlessly debated by the most ancient philosophers: from such a unity as we have declared The One to be, how does anything at all come into substantial existence, any multiplicity, dyad, or number? Why has the Primal not remained self-gathered so that there be none of this profusion of the manifold which we observe in existence and yet are compelled to trace to that absolute unity?" Plotinus, *Enneads*.

10. I.e., this world.

11. Qur'an, VI, 67.

SIXTH CLASS

1. The title of this class refers to intellects. In this chapter Ibn Sina provides a definition of "complete richness" to show that the only being that is completely rich is the First Principle or God. Since by "complete richness" is meant lack of dependency on any external thing in any way, and because the First Principle or

God is the only being that enjoys complete independence from any external thing, the conclusion to be drawn is that God is the only completely rich being.

2. The present chapter is a mere conclusion of the last one; namely, it pursues the idea that God cannot depend on anything for his perfection. Therefore, God cannot intend or seek to do anything for any other beings by way of trying to complete his perfection. Compare with *al-Najāt, al-Ṭabīʿiyyāt*, bk. 3, pp. 304–8. I agree with al-Tusi that the present chapter should have been titled "A Follow-up," and the following one "Admonition," rather than the other way around. This is because this chapter continues and builds on the idea presented in the previous one; while the following chapter presents a new definition. See al-Tusi, *Commentary, Part Three*, p. 124.

3. The real king is not only that which does not depend on anything else but also that on which everything else depends and to which everything else belongs.

4. Text: *yanbaghī*. See Analysis, note 77.

5. Thus, an analysis of the notion of generosity reveals that generosity consists of three elements: (1) providing a benefit, (2) not just any benefit, but a benefit that must be or that is a true benefit to that to which it is given, and (3) for nothing in return. See al-Tusi, *Commentary, Part Three*, p. 125.

6. Text: *jād*.

7. This is because, like all exalted beings, God has no end in what is inferior to him, and, because there is nothing above him, it follows he cannot have an end in anything.

8. This title also includes the phrase "and in a Certain Manuscript: Completion," but it does not specify the manuscript.

9. In other words, the Rich performs good acts, not for anything that he seeks for himself or for anything else, but as a result of being necessitated to do that by the nature of such acts.

10. I.e., God.

11. See chapter 22 of the Seventh Class. For a more detailed view of Ibn Sina's concept of providence, see *Al-Shifāʾ, al-Ilāhiyyāt*, bk. 9, ch. 6, p. 415.

12. The reference here is to the Third Class, chapters 28 and 29.

13. That is, permanently so.

14. This chapter attempts to show that the final cause or objective of the celestial motion is imitation of the celestial intellects.

15. Goichon erroneously gives the following title to this chapter: "Sur la multiplicité des intelligences qu'imitent les âmes célestes" (Regarding the multiplicity of intelligences that imitate the celestial souls). Goichon, *Livre des directives et remarques*, p. 405. However, according to Ibn Sina, the celestial souls imitate the celestial intelligences, not the other way around. Therefore, the phrase

"intelligences qu'imitent les âmes célestes" (intelligences that imitate the celestial souls) should read instead "intelligences qui sont imités par les âmes célestes" (intelligences that are imitated by the celestial souls).

16. That is, the side that exerts infinite movements on the larger body.

17. Text: *fa-yaṣīr al-jānib al-ākhar* (and hence becomes the other side).

18. I.e., the side that exerts finite movements on the smaller body.

19. Since it exerts finite movements on the smaller body.

20. This is because the body that is supposed to be infinite involves both infinity and finitude.

21. See chapter 19 of the present class. See also Goichon, *Livre des directives et remarques*, p. 454, note 7.

22. According to al-Tusi, chapter 10 of this class is the source of this delusion. *Commentary, Part Three*, p. 176.

23. The heavenly soul, which is a corporeal force, is the proximate or immediate mover of the heavens in the sense of being its agent cause. The separate heavenly intellects (with the First Intelligence being the primary intellect) are remote movers of the heavens and move it as its final cause.

24. That is, the third.

25. Text: *ʿalā anna* (since; even though).

26. According to al-Tusi, this reference is to the Fifth Class. Al-Tusi, *Commentary, Part Three*, p. 183.

27. Also, according to al-Tusi, the reference is to the First Class. Al-Tusi, *Commentary, Part Three*, p. 183).

28. That is, the celestial souls.

29. That is, the separate intellects.

30. This is because of the already mentioned simultaneous presence of the absence of void in the container and the existence of the contained. Therefore, if the absence of void in the container is necessary with the necessity of the container, it would follow that the existence of the contained is also necessary with the necessity of the container. But this is impossible because it was shown to be possible rather than necessary with it.

31. That is, the same as the answer given in the last chapter.

32. This is the last in the series of chapters intended as preparation for demonstrating the existence of the separate intellects.

33. These forms or perfections are the souls of the bodies.

34. Text: *wa-amkan an taṣdur ʿanh maʿlulātuh* (it is possible that Its effects come from it).

35. Some of Ibn Sina's predecessors similarly felt the need to delegate creative power from the One to subsidiary Intellects. See Plato, *Timaeus*, 28a and Plotinus,

Enneads, V.2. Aquinas, on the other hand, argues that only God creates, sometimes using creatures as instruments. See Thomas Aquinas, *Summa,* I.45.5, resp:

> And thus Avicenna asserted that the first separate substance created by God created another after itself, and the substance of the world and its soul; and that the substance of the world creates the matter of inferior bodies. And in the same manner the Master says (Sent. iv, D, 5) that God can communicate to a creature the power of creating, so that the latter can create ministerially, not by its own power. But such a thing cannot be, because the secondary instrumental cause does not participate the action of the superior cause, except inasmuch as by something proper to itself it acts dispositively to the effect of the principal agent.
>
> Trans. Fathers of the English Dominican Province,
> http://www.newadvent.org/summa/.

SEVENTH CLASS

1. This class is a group of ideas concerning things separate from matter, hence the title "Abstraction."

2. The text here reflects with clarity the Neoplatonist emanation tendency that heavily influenced Ibn Sina and al-Farabi before him.

3. The acquired intellect is a perfection that occurs to the rational soul when it actually acquires the intelligibles, which then become constantly represented in it and viewed by it whenever it wishes without the need for any further acquisition. Ibn Sina describes this perfection as "a light upon a light" (Third Class, p. 391).

4. See Third Class, for example, chapter 13.

5. See Goichon, *Livre des directives et remarques,* p. 438, note 3.

6. Text: *istithnāʾ.*

7. That is, it is not fatigued by the repetition of acts. Ibn Sina, however, does not claim that this is always the case, but only that it is often so. He probably intends to say that the rational power gets fatigued not in itself but in its operations when it uses the imagination (a bodily organ) and when the imagination gets fatigued.

8. The purpose of this chapter is to show that rational powers can know themselves, because they can grasp themselves without the need for any intermediary instruments. This is because their acts need not be by virtue of instruments. This is contrary to nonrational powers which cannot know themselves because, in order to know themselves, they would need to have intermediary instruments

between themselves as knowers and themselves as known objects, but by nature they cannot have such intermediary instruments and they cannot act except by virtue of instruments. See al-Tusi, *Commentary, Part Three*, pp. 251–52; see also Goichon, *Livre des directives et remarques*, p. 439, note 2.

9. That is, the above arguments.

10. I have replaced Dunya's reading of this sentence as "al-jawhar al-ʿaqliyy mithāluh an yaʿqil bi-dhātih" (which may be translated as "the rational substance is of the type that knows by itself") with Forget's reading: "al-jawhar al-ʿaqliyy minnā lah an yaʿqil bi-dhātih." *Kitāb al-Ishārāt wal-tanbīhāt*, p. 178.

11. That is, because it is simple, it cannot be composed of matter and form.

12. Which is a contradiction in terms.

13. Text: *yajtamiʿ, fīhā* (formed in it, or formed in them). "Formed in it" could refer to the rational power, "formed in them" to their subjects, i.e., to the subjects of the accidents. Since Ibn Sina's purpose here is to show that the rational power cannot be the subject of any composition, I took *fīhā* to refer to the rational power.

14. This seems to be a reference to the Peripatetics. For Aristotle's theory of cognition in which this view is expressed, see Aristotle, *De Anima*, 430a: "Mind is itself thinkable in exactly the same way as its objects are. For (a) in the case of objects which involve no matter, what thinks and what is thought are identical; for speculative knowledge and its object are identical. (Why mind is not always thinking we must consider later.) (b) In the case of those which contain matter each of the objects of thought is only potentially present." *De Anima*, trans. J. A. Smith, in *The Basic Works of Aristotle*, ed. Richard McKeon (New York: Random House, 1941).

15. Al-Tusi correctly points out that in his book, *al-Mabdaʾ wal-Maʿād*, Ibn Sina presents this Peripatetic view, which he will now criticize here. See *Commentary, Part Three*, p. 268. It must be remembered that in that book Ibn Sina expressed the wish simply to provide an exposition of the "real Peripatetic" view rather than his own, collecting what Peripatetics dispersed, clarifying what they concealed, declaring what they kept hidden, and simplifying what they left complex (*al-Mabdaʾ wal-Maʿād*, p. 1). That is why the view under consideration was presented there without criticism.

16. Porphyry (234–304 c.e.), a Neoplatonist philosopher who was born in Tyre, Phoenicia, in the south of present-day Lebanon, and was said to have died in Rome, where he had studied with Plotinus. He is best known for editing Plotinus's *Enneads* and writing the *Isagoge*, which has been considered an introduction to Aristotle's logical works and focuses on the five predicables or universal terms (genus, species, difference, property, and common accident). For elaboration on these terms, the importance of Porphyry's *Isagoge* in Arabic logic, and the respect in which Ibn Sina disagreed with Porphyry, see Inati, "Logic," pp. 814–17.

17. Text: *Ḥashf kulluh.*

18. Therefore, there is no union between the two things.

19. Text: *Al-jalāya al-ʿaqliyya* (rational manifestations). See Goichon, *Livre des directives et remarques*, p. 450, note 1.

20. See Fourth Class, chapter 28.

21. These are the celestial substances, which necessarily follow from God and come to know him only by virtue of his illumination. Though Ibn Sina attributes to them no yearning for anything, including God, he refers to them as lovers of God and describes them as "sincere, saintly devotees." Eighth Class in *Ibn Sina and Mysticism*, p. 79.

22. The reference is to the present class, chs. 7–8.

23. This is the end of the delusion to which Ibn Sina will now respond with a remark.

24. What is intended by this chapter is that that whose existence is necessary knows particular things in a universal manner, as do other intellects, while sensitive powers know them in a particular manner.

25. Text: "Fa-innah lais kawnuh qādiran mutaʿalliqan bih al-iḍāfa al-mutaʿayyina taʿalluqan mā lā budd minh" (which may be read as "Its having power is not such that the individual relations depend on it in some unavoidable manner"). However, Ibn Sina's idea, as shown in the following sentence in the text, is that a being's essential power does not depend on any particular relation, rather than the other way around. Perhaps *bih al-iḍāfa* was intended as *bil-iḍāfa.*

26. Text: *wa* (and).

27. Text: *wa* (and).

28. Text: *idhā* (if). Forget's reading here p. 185, *idh* (since), is more appropriate to the meaning.

29. See Fourth Class, chapter 10. Some medieval Latin authors saw themselves as diverging from Ibn Sina's theory of God's knowledge of particulars, holding that God's knowledge and providence must extend to particulars. See, for example, Thomas Aquinas, *Summa*, I.14.11, resp:

> On the other hand, others have said that God knows singular things by the application of universal causes to particular effects. But this will not hold; forasmuch as no one can apply a thing to another unless he first knows that thing; hence the said application cannot be the reason of knowing the particular, for it presupposes the knowledge of singular things. Therefore it must be said otherwise, that, since God is the cause of things by His knowledge, as stated above (Article 8), His knowledge extends as far as His causality extends. Hence as the active power of

God extends not only to forms, which are the source of universality, but also to matter, as we shall prove further on (44, 2), the knowledge of God must extend to singular things, which are individualized by matter.
Trans. Fathers of the English Dominican Province,
http://www.newadvent.org /summa/.

30. Chapters 22–27 of this class are a revised version of a text translated by Shams C. Inati in *An Anthology of Philosophy in Persia*, ed. Sayyed Hossein Nasr and Mehdi Aminrazavi (London: Tauris, 2008), 1:289–92.

From here to the end of the present class, the focus will be on the concepts of providence, goodness, and evil by way of offering a theodicy.

31. The concept of providence was briefly discussed in the Sixth Class, chapter 9. For a discussion of Ibn Sina's concept of providence, see Shams Inati, *The Problem of Evil: Ibn Sina's Theodicy* (Binghamton: Global, 2000), ch. 5.

32. Text: *lahā* (to them). I have replaced "to them" with "from them." Anyone familiar with the material preceding this statement, and the material in *al-Shifāʾ*, *al-Ilāhiyyāt*, bk. 9, ch. 6, understands that in this sentence Ibn Sina is repeating his view that something like fire cannot be itself unless it is such that accidental evil proceeds from it under certain circumstances, i.e., when it is placed in contact with a combustible element. The substitution of "from them" for "to them" is therefore necessary to render Ibn Sina's meaning.

33. Text: *lahā* (to them). I have also replaced "to them" here with "from them" for the same reason given in the previous note.

34. The opponent's delusion as presented here is this: Evil among people cannot be described as rare the way Ibn Sina describes it, since the majority of people are overcome by different forms of evil, including ignorance, desire, or anger.

35. Ibn Sina is reiterating here the Qur'anic assertion: "wa-raḥmatī wasiʿat kull shayʾ [My Mercy embraces all things]." Qur'an, VII, 156.

36. Text: *wa* (and).

37. I have replaced Dunya's reading, *furriʿʿanh*, with that of Forget, *furrigh ʿanh*. *Kitāb al-Ishārāt wal-tanbīhāt*, p. 188.

38. That is, the second division, in other words, the sublunary sphere.

39. That is, as mixed with evil.

40. Text: *jiha*, literally, side, direction.

41. Text: *jiha*, literally, side, direction.

42. Text: *min* (from).

43. In contrast to the class of punishment just discussed whose principle is from within.

44. Text: *min asbāb al-qadar* (from the causes of destiny, among the causes of destiny).

45. Text: *al-gharaḍ al-ʿām* (the general purpose).

46. I have substituted *aḍḍādihā* (their contraries) for *amthālihā* (their like).

47. That is, in the first part of *al-Ishārāt*. See *Remarks and Admonitions, Part One*, pp. 21–34, 118–28.

Bibliography

WORKS BY IBN SINA

Aḍḥawiyya fī al-Maʿād li-Ibn Sīna. Ed. Hasan Asi. Beirut: al-Muʾassasa al-Jāmiʿiyya lil-Dirāsāt wal-Nashr wal-Tawzīʿ, 1987.

Al-Ishārāt wal-Tanbīhāt. French trans. Amélie Marie Goichon. Livre des directives et remarques. Paris: J. Vrin, 1948.

Al-Ishārāt wal-Tanbīhāt. 4 vols. Ed. Sulayman Dunya. Cairo: Dār al-Maʿārif, Part Two, 1992; Part Three, 1985.

Al-Mabdaʾ wal-Maʿād. Ed. B. A. Nurani. Tehran: Muʾassat Mutalaʿat Islami Danshkah, 1984.

Al-Najāt, al-Ṭabīʿiyyāt. Ed. Majid Fakhry. Beirut: Dār al-Afāq al-Jadīda, 1985.

Al-Shifāʾ, al-Ilāhiyyāt. Ed. Muhammad Yusuf Musa, Sulayman Dunya, and Said Zayid. Cairo: Al-Hayʿa al-ʿAmma li-Shuʾun al-Maṭabiʿ al-Amīriyya, 1960.

Al-Shifāʾ, al-Manṭiq, al-Madkhal. Ed. I. Madkour, G. Anawati, M. al-Khudairi, and F. al-Ahwani. Cairo: Al-Maṭbaʿa al-Amīriyya, 1952.

Al-Shifāʾ, aṭ-Ṭabīʿiyyāt, Part One. Ed. Said Zayid. Cairo: Al-Hayʿa al-Maṣriyya al-ʿĀmma lil-Kitāb, 1983.

Al-Shifāʾ, Metaphysics, Ninth Treatise, "On Providence: Showing the Manner of the Entry of Evil in Divine Predetermination." Trans. Shams C. Inati in An Anthology of Philosophy in Persia, vol. 1, ed. Sayyed Hossein Nasr and Mehdi Aminrazavi. New York: Oxford University Press, 1999.

Ibn Sina and Mysticism: Remarks and Admonitions, Part Four. Trans. Shams C. Inati. London: Kegan Paul, 1996.

Ibn Sina Remarks and Admonitions, Part One: Logic. Trans. Shams C. Inati. Toronto: Pontifical Institute for Mediaeval Studies, 1984.

Kitāb al-Ishārāt wa-al-Tanbīhāt. Ed. Jacobus Forget. Leyden: Brill, 1892.

Manṭiq al-Mashriqiyyīn. Cairo: Al-Maktaba al-Salafiyya, 1910.

The Metaphysics of the Healing. Trans. Michael E. Marmura. Provo, UT: Brigham Young University Press, 2005.

ʿUyūn al-Ḥikma. Ed. Abd ar-Rahman Badawi. Cairo: al-Maʿhad al-ʿIlmī al-Faransī lil-Athār al-Sharqiyya, 1954.

OTHER SOURCES

al-Farabi, Abu Nasr. *Arāʾ Ahl al-Madīna al-Fāḍila*. Ed. Albert Nusir Nadir. Beirut: Dār al-Mashriq, 1996.

Al-Ghazali. *Tahāfut al-Falāsifa*. Ed. Sulayman Dunya. Cairo: Dār al-maʿārif, 1972.

al-Tusi. *Commentary*. In Ibn Sina, *Al-Ishārāt wal-Tanbīhāt*. Ed. Sulayman Dunya. Cairo: Dār al-Maʿārif, 1992.

Aristotle. *The Complete Works of Aristotle*. Rev. Oxford ed. and trans. Jonathan Barnes. Princeton: Princeton University Press, 1995.

Averroes. *Averroes' Commentary on Plato's Republic*. Hebrew ed. and trans. E. I. J. Rosenthal. Cambridge: Cambridge University Press, 1969.

Hourani, George F. "Averroes on Good and Evil." *Studia Islamica* 16 (1962): 13–40.

Inati, Shams C. "Logic." In *History of Islamic Philosophy*, ed. Seyyed Hossein Nasr and Oliver Leaman, 814–17. London: Routledge, 1996.

Jurjani, Ali Ibn Muhammad. *Kitāb al-Taʿrīfāt*. Beirut: Maktabat Lubnān, 1969.

McGinnis, Jon. "Arabic and Islamic Natural Philosophy and Natural Science." *Stanford Encyclopedia of Philosophy*. 2006. http://plato.stanford.edu.

Murray, Michael. "Leibniz on the Problem of Evil." *Stanford Encyclopedia of Philosophy* (online), 2005.

Nurani, B. Abdallah. *Al-Mabdaʾ wal-Maʿād*. Tehran: Muʾassat Mutalaʿat Islami Danshkah, 1984.

Plato. *The Collected Dialogues*. Ed. Edith Hamilton and Huntingdon Cairns. Princeton: Princeton University Press, 1963.

Plotinus. *The Enneads*. Rev. B. S. Page. Trans. Stephen MacKenna. London: Faber and Faber, 1956.

Rosenthal, E. I. J. *Averroes' Commentary on Plato's Republic*. Cambridge: Cambridge University Press, 1969.

Index

Printed in the USA
CPSIA information can be obtained
at www.ICGtesting.com
LVHW050854280124
770124LV00078B/179/J